P9-DDU-341

Who's That in the White House?

The
Formative
Years

1829 to 1857

ANDREW
JACKSON

MARTIN
VAN BUREN

WILLIAM HENRY
HARRISON

JOHN
TYLER

JAMES K.
POLK

ZACHARY
TAYLOR

MILLARD
FILLMORE

FRANKLIN
PIERCE

by Rose Blue and Corinne J. Naden

RAINTREE
STECK-VAUGHN
PUBLISHERS
The Steck-Vaughn Company
Austin, Texas

To the memory of Mary Lee Graeme and to Rose's mom,
two very gutsy ladies.

Published by Raintree Steck-Vaughn Publishers, an imprint of Steck-Vaughn Company

Publishing Director: Walter Kossmann
Editor: Shirley Shalit
Consultant: Andrew Frank, University of Florida

Project Manager: Lyda Guz
Electronic Production: Scott Melcer
Photo Editor: Margie Foster

Library of Congress Cataloging-in-Publication Data
Blue, Rose.
The formative years 1829 to 1857 / by Rose Blue and Corinne J. Naden.
p.   cm. — (Who's that in the White House?)
Includes bibliographical references and index.
Summary: Examines the lives and political careers of the presidents from Andrew Jackson through Franklin Pierce.
ISBN 0-8172-4301-1
1. Presidents — United States — Biography — Juvenile literature.   2. United States — Politics and government — 1815–1861 — Juvenile literature.   [1. Presidents.   2. United States — Politics and government — 1815–1861.]   I. Naden, Corinne J.   II. Title.   III. Series: Blue, Rose. Who's that in the White House?
E176.1.B667   1998
973.5 — dc21

97-15727
CIP   AC

Acknowledgments
The authors wish to thank Harold C. Vaughan of Fort Lee, New Jersey, for his critical reading of the manuscript. Photography credits: Cover White House Photo; Title page (all): National Portrait Gallery, Smithsonian Institution; p. 5 (left) The Granger Collection, (right) North Wind Picture Archives; p. 6 The Granger Collection; p. 7 National Portrait Gallery, Smithsonian Institution; p. 8 The Granger Collection; p. 9 White House Historical Association/Courtesy Ladies' Hermitage Association; p. 12 North Wind Picture Archives; p. 15 The Granger Collection; pp. 16, 18 Corbis-Bettman; p. 21 Courtesy Woolaroc Museum, Bartlesville, OK; p. 24 The Granger Collection; p. 25 National Portrait Gallery, Smithsonian Institution; p. 26 North Wind Pictures; p. 31 "The Reading of the Texas Declaration of Independence" Courtesy Joe Fultz; p. 35 Corbis-Bettmann; p. 37 The Granger Collection; p. 38 National Portrait Gallery, Smithsonian Institution; p. 39 Culver Pictures; p. 40 North Wind Picture Archives; p. 43 The Granger Collection; p. 45 National Portrait Gallery, Smithsonian Institution; p. 48 White House Historical Association/Courtesy Mr. John Tyler Griffin; p. 49 White House Historical Association ; p. 51 Corbis-Bettmann; p. 52 The Granger Collection; p. 53 National Portrait Gallery, Smithsonian Institution; p. 54 Culver Pictures; p. 57 White House Historical Association; p. 59 The Granger Collection; p. 62 North Wind Pictures; p. 64 The Granger Collection; p. 65 National Portrait Gallery, Smithsonian Institution; p. 66 White House Historical Association; pp. 67, 69 The Granger Collection; p. 72 National Portrait Gallery, Smithsonian Institution; p. 75 White House Historical Association; p. 76 Corbis-Bettman; p. 77 Culver Pictures; p. 78 The Granger Collection; p. 79 National Portrait Gallery, Smithsonian Institution; p. 81 White House Historical Association; p. 83 The Granger Collection; p. 84 The Kansas State Historical Society; p. 87 The Granger Collection.

Cartography: GeoSystems, Inc.

Printed and bound in the United States
1 2 3 4 5 6 7 8 9 0 LB 01 00 99 98 97

Contents

Forty Years and Growing

*I*t was the year 1829. Forty years had passed since George Washington was inaugurated as first President of the United States. Since then, five men had lived in the White House. The Union now had 24 states, and the bustling population was more than 12 million. The great experiment in self-government was up and growing. Not yet steady, perhaps, but at least starting to make it on its own. It now stretched from the busy Atlantic coast to the untamed western borders of Missouri. These were the formative years, from the seventh President to the fourteenth, from 1829 to 1857, from Andrew Jackson to Franklin Pierce.

During the formative years, it almost seemed as though the White House had a revolving front door. Did anyone want to stay? Of the eight Presidents during this period, only one—Andrew Jackson—lasted eight years. William Henry Harrison hardly had time to unpack his luggage. He died less than 31 days in office. Zachary Taylor died after one year and four months. Tyler and Fillmore, respectively, filled the remaining terms of those Presidents. Van Buren, Polk, and Pierce each managed one four-year term. Except for Jackson, historians generally do not rank these men as outstanding Presidents. That is mainly because, by and large, each of them failed to deal effectively with the issue of slavery. Left unresolved, it led, finally, to the Civil War.

The changes during what we call the formative years of the United States were not always directly connected with the office of the President. A rising feeling of sectionalism was spreading—

By the 1840s and 1850s, rural scenes, such as this one painted by Edwards Hicks of a New York farm, were being supplemented by industrial manufacturers, like this Pawtucket, Rhode Island, factory that made buttonhole cutters.

north, south, east, west, city, country, farm, factory. Economic changes in the market surely would have taken place whatever the President's name. After Jackson, no President of this era is regarded as truly influential. Yet, all eight men of the formative years hold a unique spot in history books simply because they sat in the White House—even, in some cases, for so short a time.

If the men in the White House were changing rapidly during this period, so was the country. It was, in a sense, forming itself. America was discovering its own character, shifting from Jeffersonian to Jacksonian democracy. Jefferson believed that the so-called common man had the *right to choose* his leaders from among those qualified. Jacksonians said that the common man *himself* could be the leader. That was quite a difference in philosophy.

Naturally, these lofty ideals of equality did not extend to women. That would take another century. They didn't extend to most blacks or to Native Americans either. That took the Fifteenth Amendment to the Constitution in 1870 and the Civil Rights legislation of the 1950s and 1960s.

The country was changing physically, too. Under Presidents Washington through J.Q. Adams, voters had been mainly farmers or small merchants. But by the early 1800s, cities were growing rapidly. A whole new voting power came into being. Jackson was elected in 1829 mostly by a group of voters that had simply not existed before. Its members were the emerging American working class of the cities and factories.

The West was forming its own character, too. More and more people were pushing the frontier westward toward the Pacific. They had different backgrounds and educations. But they had one common goal. They were going to tame the wilderness. The ability to survive and prosper often became more important than the conditions of one's birth—at least for a while.

The times they were a-changing. A new country was forming and it would suffer severe growing pains. The men in the White House during this period were confronted with problems that would not go away. Jackson began the formative years as the people's popular hero. Pierce ended the formative years standing in the eye of a hurricane that threatened to destroy the marvelous experiment begun nearly 70 years before.

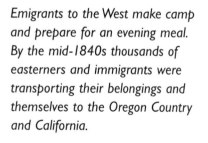

Emigrants to the West make camp and prepare for an evening meal. By the mid-1840s thousands of easterners and immigrants were transporting their belongings and themselves to the Oregon Country and California.

Chapter One

Jackson: The People's President

Andrew Jackson (1829-1837)

*I*f the formative years sig-naled a time of change, the seventh President of the United States fit right in. Andrew Jackson himself was a change from the six men who had held the job before him. Jackson was the first to be elected from a western state. Although he was born in rural South Carolina, near the North Carolina border, he went to the White House from Tennessee. The first six U.S. Presidents had come from states on the eastern coast: Washington, Jefferson, Madison, and Monroe from Virginia and John and J.Q. Adams from Massachusetts.

Jackson was different in other ways as well. He was the first national leader to come from a poor farming family and the first to be born of Irish immigrant parents. He seems to have been the first to have spent at least a part of his childhood in a log cabin.

Jackson was the first President elected with an official count of both Electoral College *and* popular votes. The U.S. Constitution calls for the states to appoint electors, known collectively as the Electoral College. These electors, not the general public, vote directly for President and vice president. A candidate can lose the popular vote but still be elected if he or she gets the majority of votes in the Electoral College. The popular vote had been counted for the first time in 1824, but that election had been decided by the House of Representatives because of a tie, with Jackson the loser. Jackson's popular vote count in the election of 1828 was 647,231.

Jackson was also the first President to spring out of bed into a hot shower! Iron pipes were installed in the White House to bring in springwater during his second term. An important presidential first, indeed!

Jackson has another distinction as well. Some historians say he is second only to George Washington, or perhaps a close third to Franklin D. Roosevelt, in the profound influence he had on the office of President of the United States.

Andrew Jackson was born on March 15, 1767, in an area that was not even a state of the Union. South Carolina would not gain statehood for 21 years. He never knew his Irish immigrant father, who died two weeks before his birth. His mother, Elizabeth, had her hands full raising him and two older brothers.

Jackson never would be a scholar, but he did learn to read and write by the time he was eight years old. He grew into a tall, freckle-faced, red-haired teenager with a trigger temper. He was strong and tough even as a youngster. Later, Jackson's extraordinary stamina and strength became the stuff of legends and earned him the nickname "Old Hickory." When the American Revolution reached the frontier, his brother Hugh was killed in battle and his brother Robert, just 16 years old, died of wounds and smallpox. Thirteen-year-old Andrew, slashed by a British officer's bayonet and also suffering from smallpox, survived. So did his hatred of the British.

In this Currier & Ives lithograph, teenaged Andrew Jackson is shown being slashed by a British officer for refusing to clean the officer's boots.

As if young Andrew had not experienced enough sorrow and suffering, he was soon left completely alone in the world. His mother died of an undiagnosed fever and was buried in an unmarked grave. But the tough times only made Andrew tougher. After his mother's death, he went to Salisbury, North Carolina, and studied law. In 1788, he became public prosecutor for the Western District of North Carolina, now Tennessee. The small settlement of Nashville, far from civilization and in the midst of hostile Indian territory, suited the temperament of this wild, somewhat reckless, and very inexperienced young lawyer.

Just *how* wild and reckless? Jackson's fiery temper kept him on a short fuse, and he was quick to challenge all who crossed him. A rebel with or without a cause, this reckless hothead fell in love with beautiful Rachel Robards who had separated from her husband, Lewis. Believing her divorce to have been granted, Rachel and Jackson were married in August 1791. Alas for the newlyweds, the divorce was not actually granted until 1793. Jackson learned the truth that December, and they were remarried in January.

Living together without being married, at least in the upper social ranks of society, was not dismissed lightly in the eighteenth century. Far worse, however, was the charge of adultery. Even though Andrew and Rachel had believed her divorce to be valid, she was still considered by many to be an adulteress. Her

Rachel Donelson Jackson

shame was gleefully and maliciously discussed over many an afternoon teacup! But woe to anyone who mentioned it in front of Andrew Jackson! To his sorrow, John Sevier found that out. One day in 1803, the Tennessee governor was standing on the courthouse steps bragging about what he had done for the newly formed state. When Jackson started to do a little bragging himself, Sevier said, "I know of no great service you have rendered, except taking a trip…with another's man's wife."

Jackson immediately hit him over the head with a stick and challenged Sevier to a duel. Sevier was lucky. His horse ran away and no one fired a shot.

Charles Dickinson wasn't so fortunate. After twice making remarks about Rachel, he found himself facing her husband with raised dueling pistols. Jackson was hit in the chest. With his incredible stamina, he staggered a bit but did not fall down. Instead, he raised his gun and aimed. Dickinson stared in disbelief. How could his shot have missed? Horrified by that thought, he took a step backward. But this was against the very precise rules of dueling, and a fatal error. Because his opponent had not yet fired, Dickinson had to step back to his original mark. Jackson took aim and Dickinson died a slow, agonizing death. As for Jackson, he would live in frequent pain the rest of his life because the bullet in his chest was too close to his heart to be safely removed.

The mix-up over their marriage brought Jackson great pain, but it was worse for Rachel. Although deeply in love, she could not overcome the bitterness and sorrow that the ugly rumors caused throughout the rest of her life. Rachael died three months before her husband took office, and Jackson forever blamed the death of his "dear saint" on those who spread the vicious gossip.

Tennessee became a state in 1796. Supposedly, Jackson is credited with naming it. By then, he had become a practiced lawyer of some wealth. In time he acquired the Hermitage, outside Nashville, which became the Jacksons' beloved home. The extensive gardens and beautiful old mansion, rebuilt after a fire in 1834, is now a national landmark.

Jackson became a judge advocate in the county militia. He was skilled with a gun and hated the British and all Native Americans. Although his anti-British feelings stemmed from the Revolution, his unreasonable hatred of all Native Americans was surely his least endearing quality. Throughout his lifetime, his treatment of Native Americans was often shameful.

With statehood, Jackson was elected from Tennessee to the House of Representatives. Next, he spent a year in the Senate, returning home to sit on the state superior court. During the War of 1812, by then a major general in the U.S. Volunteers, he was anxious to fight the British. Without waiting for official sanction, he organized a division and set off for the South. President Madison ordered him home. Livid with anger at the command, Jackson nevertheless led his men back through 500 miles of wilderness. After the trek, his troops said he was "tough as hickory." So that's what they began calling him—Old Hickory. He had worked hard at earning that nickname.

The year after he was ordered back, Jackson got into another of his famous fights. It did not concern Rachel, however. This time, Thomas Hart Benton, congressman from North Carolina, made some uncomplimentary remarks about Jackson. Benton should have known better. Andrew Jackson was hardly the sort to take criticism lightly. One day in 1813, he saw Benton and his brother, Jesse, enter a hotel in Nashville. He followed them carrying a horsewhip, which he intended to use. After the fracas, Jackson wound up with two bullet wounds and a shattered shoulder. Old Hickory refused to have the arm amputated. Later, Jackson and Benton actually became friends.

His shoulder had not yet healed when Jackson heard about trouble with the Creek Indians in Alabama. Never one to miss a fight if it concerned Native Americans, he rose from his bed and went into battle. The fighting dragged on into 1814, but Old Hickory was successful. Perhaps too successful. He imposed such a harsh treaty on the Creeks that the federal government canceled most of its severe terms.

Despite his attitude toward Native Americans, the government in Washington could not ignore Jackson's military skill. The War of 1812 was still raging in late 1814. But it had now shifted to

Andrew Jackson on his white horse is shown, in this color lithograph, encouraging his soldiers during the Battle of New Orleans.

the South, and the British stood ready to capture the city of New Orleans. Under the circumstances, it seemed natural to send Jackson to the rescue.

General Jackson decided on the "long route" to New Orleans. On the way, he stopped in Spanish Florida and routed the British from Pensacola. No one, certainly not the federal government, had told him to do so. He just felt it should belong to America. Soon it did. Then, it was on to New Orleans and more hated British.

On the night of January 7, 1815, several thousand British troops were camped on a plantation outside the city. Reinforcements were to arrive in the morning, when the British would attack. Jackson was having none of that. Shouting, "They shall not sleep on our soil!" he ordered the schooner *Carolina* down the Mississippi River in darkness to shell the enemy. Shocked by the night attack, which many historians say saved the city, the British were no match for Old Hickory the next morning.

Jackson and his strange force—frontiersmen, free black Americans, some Choctaw warriors, and pirate Jean Lafitte and his crew—were overwhelmingly victorious on January 8, 1815. Historians differ about the number of casualties, but the British may have lost more than 2,000 men, whereas Americans killed and wounded numbered less than 100.

Oh, how the young nation cheered! There hadn't been such a hero since George Washington and the days of the Revolution! In a way, though, it was a strange victory. The Battle of New Orleans, which brought Jackson national fame and a path to the White House, actually took place when the war was already over! The Treaty of Ghent, more a truce than a peace treaty, had been signed on December 24, 1814. Communications being what they were in the early 1800s, Jackson, of course, did not know that.

After his victory, Jackson showed some rather shabby behavior in Spanish Florida, even though most Americans backed him. Spain was having difficulty keeping peace in eastern Florida, and most U.S. leaders had their eye on the Florida territory anyway. Native Americans from the Seminole and Creek nations clashed with U.S. troops along the border and were pushed back into Florida. However, skirmishes continued. In December 1817, President James Monroe told Jackson to keep the tribes away from the border but not to follow them if they entered Spanish forts.

President Monroe must have been a bit naive. Naturally, Old Hickory had no intention of obeying such an order. Instead, he burned a Native American village and executed some of the inhabitants because, he said, the British were aiding them. From there, he pushed on to Pensacola and ousted the Spanish governor, putting one of his own men in charge. Monroe naturally denied giving Jackson such orders, but he didn't scold him, either. The President was well aware of what a popular hero the General was. Spain officially gave up Florida in 1819, and Jackson became the territory's governor for four months in 1821.

By the time he returned to Nashville, people were talking about sending him to the White House. At first, he said that he wasn't such a fool "as to think myself fit for President of the United States." But the temptation was as hard to ignore then as it is today, so he got himself elected to the Senate and went to Washington.

In the election of 1824, no candidate won a majority of the electoral votes. Jackson led with 99, John Quincy Adams had 84, William Crawford got 41, and Henry Clay, 37. The deadlock gave the decision to the House of Representatives, which elected John Quincy Adams, with a little help from Clay, as the sixth President of the United States.

Jackson was certain he had been robbed of the election. He spent the next four years working on his campaign for the presidency. The election of 1828 was surely the start of what modern America has come to know as "mudslinging." It was unheard of up to that time in American politics, and it was also expensive. Jackson's camp spent one million dollars! His aides did everything they could to paint President Adams as an inept bungler in both national and foreign matters. They called him corrupt. Jackson followers already controlled Congress, and they kept up their attacks on the President throughout his term.

The Adams camp was hardly blameless in the campaign, however. The mudslinging became truly creative and low. The Cincinnati *Gazette* asked if the husband of a "convicted adulteress" should sit in the White House. Jackson was called a tyrant, a drunk, and a gambler. And that was for starters. There were lots of posters showing him stabbing someone in the chest with his military sword. The opposition Whig party, trying to point up Jackson's lack of education, created a symbol of the "jackass" for the Democrats. It backfired because the Democrats eagerly accepted the symbol, and the "donkey" has signified the Democratic party ever since.

But the viciousness and the mudslinging didn't really matter. Since the Battle of New Orleans, the American voter had found his democratic hero in General Andrew Jackson of Tennessee. He beat out Adams, 178 electoral votes to 83. Jackson's running mate was John C. Calhoun of South Carolina.

There was little doubt that this was a new era in American politics. Gone were the touches of aristocracy and gentility from

Old Virginia or the crisp intellectualism from Massachusetts. In their place was a plain man with firm resolve and few intellectual pursuits, easy in manner, sound in judgment, and iron in will and constitution. The contrast is evident in the opinion of the nation's third President, Thomas Jefferson. Said number three about number seven: "I feel much alarmed at the prospect of seeing General Jackson as president." Jefferson delivered that line in 1824 at the age of 81, and added: "He is one of the most unfit men I know for such a place."

Was Jefferson right? Perhaps not. Indeed, with Andrew Jackson the concept of the President's office itself did change. From Washington to J.Q. Adams, all of the first six leaders had operated on a more or less equal footing with the other two branches of government: the legislative, in the form of the Congress, and the judiciary, in the form of the courts. In fact, during those first 40 years, all six Presidents had vetoed only nine bills that Congress had passed. All were vetoed only because the Presidents believed them unconstitutional.

But Jackson saw the presidency in a different light. His idea continues to influence those who sit in the Oval Office today. The office of the President, said Jackson, *is supreme* to the legislature and the courts simply because the President is the only one of the three elected by the entire country. The President is the leader of *all* the people. Accordingly, Jackson would veto a bill if he personally thought it wrong, regardless of legality. He vetoed 12 bills during

Andrew Jackson was greeted by well-wishers at various settlements on his way from Tennessee to Washington, D.C., in 1829, for his inauguration.

his terms. He also used the "pocket veto," something no President had done before. That term applies to a law passed by Congress and sent to the President, which the President neither vetoes nor signs. He figuratively "puts it in his pocket" until Congress adjourns. The law dies.

Andrew Jackson may not have been vulgar and common as his critics claimed, but perhaps his inauguration party was! Never had there been such a sight in Washington, D.C., as the morning of March 4, 1829! The tall and white-haired, 61-year-old Jackson, in ill health but impressively garbed in black to honor his newly deceased Rachel, left Gadsby's Tavern where he had been staying. He rode his horse to the ceremony. By the time he arrived at the Capitol, people were hanging from balconies and doorways along Pennsylvania Avenue. They had slept in the streets and partied in the taverns to see "their man" get into the White House. Clerks, bankers, frontiersmen, and their families

shouted from windows and whistled and clapped as he rode stately by. Said astonished Daniel Webster, "I have never seen such a crowd before." Mannerly Chief Justice John Marshall viewed the prospect of administering the oath of office with some distaste.

Certainly the White House had never seen such a party before, and probably not since. From the inaugural address at the Capitol, the adoring crowd marched down the avenue to the reception. Before long, women were fainting and men were fighting, china was smashed, and many a muddied boot left its imprint on the White House furniture. In desperation,

The crush at the White House to celebrate Jackson's inauguration was so great that the overflow was invited to party on the lawn.

some of the attendants lured the crowd out on the lawn to drink champagne from buckets.

Through all this chaos walked the thin and pale new leader of the young nation. His ill health was obvious if anyone had cared to notice. His hands had trembled as he read his inaugural speech. At the inaugural party, he soon tired of all this boisterous admiration. The new President escaped through a back door at the White House and spent his inaugural night quietly at Gadsby's Tavern. The business of governing could wait until tomorrow.

Throughout his campaign, Jackson had often portrayed himself as a simple soldier "overwhelmed" by politicians. Once in office, however, he seemed to have no trouble taking charge. The General largely ran his own show. With the exception of Secretary of State Van Buren and Secretary of War John Eaton, Jackson generally ignored his official Cabinet. What advice he took came from his "personal consultants," known unofficially as his Kitchen Cabinet.

No children were born to Andrew and Rachel Jackson, but when Jackson moved into the White House, numerous children often visited. Most of them were relatives of Rachel's. The Jacksons had adopted one of them and named him Andrew Jackson, Jr.

Jackson has been praised or damned for introducing the spoils system into government. Actually, the system was nothing new and he did not introduce it. Presidents before him had replaced government officials when taking office. Politicians and the public think nothing of it today. And Jackson truly believed that staying in office too long could be a temptation to corruption—a familiar ring in twentieth-century politics. But when Senator William Marcy of New York announced that "to the victor belong the spoils of the enemy," it had a nasty sound to it. Indeed, the President's opponents immediately claimed he had personally introduced corruption into the central government. Jackson did replace government officials but certainly denied they were corrupt.

Perhaps not surprisingly, Jackson's first major crisis concerned an affair more passionate than political. Peggy O'Neale, the daughter of an innkeeper friend, was beautiful, spoiled, and notoriously conceited. By the time she was 16, a duel had been fought because of her, and at least one suicide attempted. Although the young lady did not find these events unflattering, she decided to settle down. She married John B. Timberlake, a navy man on what seemed to be permanent shore duty.

The circumstances surrounding Peggy O'Neale Timberlake's marriage to John Eaton, the secretary of war, finally resulted in the resignation of Jackson's Cabinet.

Presently, however, Timberlake was quite surprised to be sent out to sea. It wasn't long before the mystery was solved. Senator John Eaton of Tennessee, who apparently had some influence in government, had become quite infatuated with the young bride. The senator was soon escorting her about town.

The capital city was outraged! No one of importance would even talk to the couple. Before Jackson took office, Timberlake died at sea in 1828. No one knows how, although Washington wives were convinced he had taken his own life due to a broken heart. Jackson had his own problems. He was about to name Eaton as his secretary of war, and he certainly didn't need a scandal. Said the president-elect to Eaton, "You must shut their mouths by marrying Peggy Timberlake." That was taken care of on January 1, 1829.

One might have thought that Jackson's own marital troubles would have made him a little less naive. Naturally, the marriage did nothing at all to stop the talk. Soon *nobody* in the Cabinet was talking to anybody else, and no government work was getting done. Finally, Secretary of State Van Buren solved the problem simply by resigning. Eaton and the others took the hint and also resigned. Jackson got a new Cabinet and got down to work.

Jackson ran into trouble with his vice president, John C. Calhoun of South Carolina. The tariff of 1828, known as the "tariff of abominations," was at the heart of the trouble. It protected northern manufacturing but caused a loss of overseas shipping in the South. When another tariff was passed in 1832, South Carolina adopted the Ordinance of Nullification. It said the tariff was not binding on the state. Vice President Calhoun agreed.

Obviously, this was a challenge to the rule of the federal government. Said the President, "No state or states has a right to secede." Jackson apparently felt that South Carolina's refusal to obey a federal law, in this case pay a tariff, was a form of withdrawal from the Union. He sent a bill to Congress authorizing him to use force to save the federal government. A compromise tariff was passed, South Carolina backed down, and Jackson preserved the Union.

Jackson won the 1832 election at the top of his popularity with Martin Van Buren as his running mate. He won 219 electoral votes out of 286 and took 55 percent of the popular vote. The outstanding historical events of his second term were his war with the Bank of the United States, and on another level, his shameful treatment of the Cherokee.

Jackson had always been against the Bank of the United States, the country's only national bank. This stemmed more from prejudice than a good understanding of economics. Like many leaders in the South and West, he distrusted paper money and thought the bank—and bankers—too powerful. He criticized interest rates and policies that allowed men to make money without labor. Why entrust such large funds to just a few rich and powerful men, who were mainly from the northeast at that. But the bank was also a generally stabilizing influence on the young country's economy. Despite bank president Nicholas Biddle's attempt to change his mind, Jackson was determined to bring down the institution.

And so he did. Congress rechartered the Bank of the United States in mid-1832. A week later, Jackson vetoed the bill. "It is to be regretted that the rich and powerful too often bend the acts of government to their selfish purposes," said the President. Nicholas Biddle was outraged, but the veto held. To make sure the bank issue was dead, Jackson, in 1833, declared that no federal deposits would henceforth be made in the institution. The federal government had been the bank's largest single depositor.

Biddle was determined that the "Bank of the United States shall not break." He tightened credit and called in loans, and the bank prospered until the charter expired in 1836. After that, it became a state bank in Pennsylvania until it failed and wiped out many of its depositors.

The President won but inflation followed. Inflation occurs when there is an oversupply of money and a limited supply of consumer goods. The prices of goods and services go up. High inflation can cause severe economic problems. Jackson's victory, if not economically sound, was political maneuvering at its best. He called the bank a monopoly, which was untrue; it made only 20 percent of the country's bank loans. But the charge made Jackson look like a true champion of equality for the "common people."

Actually, Jackson *was* a true champion of equality, but it was for the "common *white* people." He had little sympathy for those in slavery, although like many an astute politician he could see the signs of trouble coming. Nat Turner's Rebellion, a slave uprising in Virginia in 1831, was the most prominent of the early warnings.

The second major historical event of Jackson's second term concerned the Cherokee. Nowhere is his prejudice against Native Americans more evident than with the Cherokee and the forced migration known as the Trail of Tears. Soon after Jackson took office, the government started a migration policy for Native Americans that went on for ten years. It was said to "save the tribes from extinction." Its true purpose was removal of all Native Americans to reservations west of the Mississippi. This, of course,

Known as the Trail of Tears, about 70,000 Indians from the southeastern United States were forced to move to Indian Territory (now Oklahoma) between 1830 and 1842.

left all their lands east of the Mississippi open to white settlers. Only a few tribes resisted. Sauk and Fox Chief Black Hawk led an open rebellion in present-day Wisconsin in 1832, but it was easily put down by government troops. The Seminoles fought the U.S. Army in Florida from 1835 to 1842. Their rebellion cost the United States a great deal of money and nearly destroyed the Seminoles.

But the Cherokee in Georgia were different. They had adapted well to the new settlers, convinced it was the only way to survive. They had long been farmers and became cattle ranchers and were the first Native Americans to develop a written language. They drafted a constitution within the state of Georgia. The United States recognized the Cherokee nation in 1828, but Georgia did not. It passed a law claiming all Cherokee lands in the state. Chief Justice John Marshall declared the Georgia law unconstitutional. Georgia ignored Marshall and forced the Cherokee to leave. Jackson, instead of upholding the Supreme Court, did nothing. In fact, it is said that he remarked, "Marshall has made his decision. Now let him enforce it."

No one else did anything about this injustice either, with the honorable exception of Henry Clay of Kentucky, who was not even involved in the evacuation. He gave an impassioned speech in Congress on the evil being done. No one listened. And so in 1835 began the long march of the Cherokee from Georgia to Oklahoma—the Trail of Tears. Four thousand Native Americans died of starvation and disease on the long, torturous move. Few lifted a hand in protest or help. This was not a proud moment in American history.

At 70 years old, Andrew Jackson left office and went back to his beloved Hermitage. Unfortunately, he nearly lost his home due to the astounding incompetence of his adopted son, Andrew junior, who was supposed to be managing the place, but instead mismanaged it, including neglecting to pay the taxes. The state of Tennessee was proud enough of their native son, however, to forget about the taxes and allow the General to retain his home.

Long in bad health, Jackson was perky enough to choose James Knox Polk for the Democratic presidential candidate in 1844, but the following year, on June 8, he fainted. After a spoonful of brandy, he revived, but shortly after, with Andrew junior at his side, the General died.

Old Hickory had brought in the Jacksonian Era, but it did not die with him. It would last until the administration of Abraham Lincoln (1861–1865), who used his own presidential power to preserve the Union.

Was Andrew Jackson a great President or just a great politician? Certainly he was the latter. He seemed to understand what most Americans were feeling. He spoke to the people. Undoubtedly, he made a change in the office of President of the United States. It would never be the same again. He used the role of chief executive not merely to carry out policy but to *make* policy. He was not a partner with other government branches, he was the leader.

In a young, forming country of individualists, Jackson could "out-individual" anyone. He was a national democratic hero. But, of course, he was not democratic at all. His concept of equality and liberty applied to whites, and generally white men only at that. He did bring in the idea that "common people" could run for office. But for Jackson, "common people" meant white men, generally poor and rural. He destroyed the Bank of the United States, setting the stage for economic depression. Whether he actually introduced the spoils system or not, he allowed into government a flow of unqualified people who served only as a payback favor. That unfortunate practice is entrenched in American government today.

For all that and despite his undesirable qualities, historians consider Andrew Jackson to have been a very influential, if not great President. He did make a difference. His presidency was a kind of turning point in the development of American democracy. Jackson saw himself as acting for all the people, and he did woo all kinds of Americans, from poor farmers to rich planters. He himself had humble origins, but he became a wealthy lawyer, cotton planter, and slave owner. Jackson understood the way people felt about issues and he acted on those feelings. He was a giant in his influence on the way the system worked. His role as President ended years of strong congressional leadership and led directly to the concept of the U.S. presidency as it is practiced today. The White House after General Andrew Jackson would never be quite the same again.

Names in the News in Jackson's Time

Nicholas Biddle (1786–1844):

Arrogant but brilliant banker from prominent Philadelphia family; director (1823) of U.S. Bank at age 37. Believed strong national bank to be basis of a sound economy. Fought and lost bank battle with Jackson. Resigned and retired in 1839.

Black Hawk (1767–1838):

Native American chieftain, born near Rock Island, Illinois. Black Hawk War of 1831 ended in victory by U.S. Army. Given audience with President Jackson (1833).

John Henry Eaton (1790–1856):

U.S. senator from Tennessee (1818–1829); U.S. secretary of war (1829–1831) under Jackson; governor of Florida (1834–1836); U.S. minister to Spain (1836–1840). Married Peggy O'Neale on Jackson's request after his affair caused turmoil in the President's Cabinet.

Roger Brooke Taney (1777–1864):

Maryland-born lawyer/adviser to Jackson during U.S. Bank conflict; secretary of treasury (1833–1834); nominated by Jackson to succeed Chief Justice John Marshall on Supreme Court (1836); associated with Dred Scott decision (1857). Slave Scott sought freedom on grounds he now resided in free territory. Court ruled Scott not a citizen and so had no standing in court.

Nat Turner (1800–1831):

Virginia-born slave leader, religious crusader. Plotted and led slave uprising (1831). Captured, convicted, and hanged (November 11, 1831).

In this 1828 cartoon of Jackson destroying the Bank of the United States, Nicholas Biddle, in a top hat, represents Pennsylvania.

Chapter Two

Master Politician Van Buren

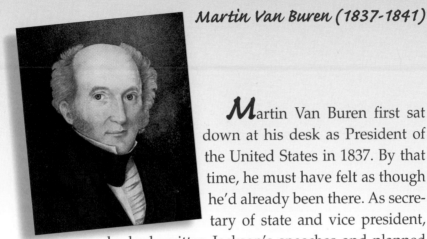

Martin Van Buren (1837-1841)

$\mathcal{M}$artin Van Buren first sat down at his desk as President of the United States in 1837. By that time, he must have felt as though he'd already been there. As secretary of state and vice president, he had written Jackson's speeches and planned his campaigns. He built the Democratic party machine. He delivered the all-important New York State vote that helped to elect Jackson. Now it was his turn.

Van Buren wasn't a genius or a great physical specimen. He was a smallish man, with a receding hairline and curly, mutton-chop sideburns. But in politics, what mattered was his uncanny sense of government. Not only did he see what had to be done, but he knew how to do it.

If Andrew Jackson was a great politician, then the man who followed him was a master. In fact, Van Buren is often called just that—the country's first national master politician.

Martin Van Buren was called other names as well. He was Little Van because he was only five feet six inches tall. Later in life, he became the "Red Fox of Kinderhook," a reference to both his hometown and his political genius. Not all this, of course, was always complimentary.

The third of five children, Little Van was a farmer's son. He was born on December 5, 1782, in the village of Kinderhook, east of the Hudson River in southeastern New York. He is buried there as well. His Dutch parents were Abraham and Maria Hoes Van Buren. His father, a farmer who also ran a tavern and fought in the American Revolution, owned slaves.

Van Buren never claimed to have a great mind and indeed had only a few years of schooling at a second-rate academy. But at around the age of 14, he became interested in politics and found work in a local law firm. The soon-to-be lawyer got his political feet wet in 1800 by campaigning for Thomas Jefferson. He returned to Kinderhook and was admitted to the bar in 1803. Four years later he married a distant relative, Hannah Hoes. The couple had four sons. Abraham would become his father's secretary in the White House, but Hannah Van Buren died long before her husband became President.

Little Van was elected to the New York State Senate in 1812. He opposed the creation of the U.S. Bank and was one of the first legislators in the nation to sponsor a bill that would stop sending people to prison for debt. It was not uncommon at the time to jail those who could not pay their bills. That made it difficult to earn a dollar and, of course, usually took away any chance to pay the bills at all. Van Buren supported the country's involvement in the War of 1812 against the British, was in favor of revising the New York State constitution, and approved the construction of the Erie Canal.

The first barges through the Erie Canal in October 1825 were greeted by enthusiastic spectators along the way.

The first great constructed waterway in the United States, the Erie Canal linked New York City via the Hudson River with the Great Lakes. In so doing, it opened the country to shipping. In 1817, New York Governor DeWitt Clinton announced construction of a canal, 363 miles long, 40 feet wide, and 4 feet deep. It ran from Buffalo to Albany on the upper Hudson River. There were no roads in the area and everything needed for the job had to be hauled in along the trails by men and horses. The Erie Canal was opened on October 25, 1825, by the canal boat *Seneca Chief.* The effect on the Midwest was startling. Settlers and shipping poured westward. Freight rates from Buffalo to New York City went from $100 a ton by land to $10 a ton by canal. But the biggest effect was on New York City. It became the major port in the land and one of the greatest in the world.

During Van Buren's second state senate term, he became the state attorney general and in his quiet way, began to take over control of New York's Republican wing known as the Bucktails. They thoroughly backed Jefferson's strong faith in democracy, states' rights, and commitment to civil liberties. It is here that Van Buren first made use of the friendly press. With his political influence, he was able to make sure that important posts on the Albany *Argus* newspaper were held by Van Buren admirers. In that way, he was certain of almost solid backing for his causes. He did not forget this lesson when he got to Washington.

Van Buren went to the U.S. Senate in 1821, where he supported states' rights, opposed a strong central government, and was against the extension of the slave trade and the importing of slaves into Florida. The Senate advanced his career to be sure, but what was he losing? He already held a good deal of political power in his own home state. And until 1860, New York State alone contained one-seventh of the entire population of the United States! The Red Fox of Kinderhook was not about to give up his influence at home, no matter where he was. So, he cooperated with New York City's political machine, known as Tammany Hall, and put together his own party machine, called the Albany Regency. It ran campaigns, made state policy, and with threats, gifts, and bribes kept those in line who might stray from the party. Martin the master politician was in control.

But Van Buren made a rare error in the 1824 presidential election campaign. He also made a masterful recovery. There were four presidential candidates that year—John Quincy Adams, Andrew Jackson, John C. Calhoun of South Carolina, and William H. Crawford of Georgia. Van Buren backed Crawford, but Adams got the presidency. Immediately, Van Buren united the three losers. His idea was to package the forceful personality and new popularity of General Jackson and sell it to a new Democratic party for the next election. This drive would be spearheaded by New York and its new governor—Van Buren himself. He resigned from the Senate in 1828 and successfully ran for governor.

Although the 1828 campaign marked the start of low and dirty politics in America, it worked. Jackson entered the White House in 1829 and Van Buren got the governor's chair in Albany, for about two months. Jackson, not surprisingly, named Van Buren secretary of state and he became, also not surprisingly, the most influential man in the President's Cabinet.

Martin Van Buren was a skillful secretary of state. Cordial and discreet, he was a gentle and amiable fellow who enjoyed fine wines and impeccable attire. He was responsible for much of Jackson's success in foreign affairs. He also worked hard to support the President's national legislation. Of course, he was not above helping himself in the bargain. Van Buren wanted to be vice president for Jackson's second term, so he pulled a neat trick to get the current vice president, John C. Calhoun, out of the way. Calhoun and Jackson were now on opposite sides anyway, because South Carolina said it would not pay federal tariffs and Calhoun agreed. This led to the "nullification crisis." Did a state's lawmakers have the right to ignore federal law if they thought such law to be against the state's best interests? Jackson said no when he came to office. But when he faced so much Southern opposition, he shifted a bit. He declared the federal tariffs to be "temporary." This caused South Carolina—and Calhoun—to calm down, believing, incorrectly, that Jackson would allow the state to take action against the tariff.

But "calmness" wasn't in Van Buren's best interests. Friction, however, was. So, Van Buren gently reminded the President that Calhoun had opposed the General's military operations in Florida back in 1818. That did it. Calhoun was on the way out. It didn't hurt that Van Buren also tactfully resigned from Jackson's Cabinet to ease the crisis over the Eaton affair. Van Buren got the nod for the number two spot.

After a short stint as minister to Great Britain, Van Buren came home to be Jackson's running mate in the campaign of 1832. Four years later he was running for the top spot himself.

For all intents, the country now had a two-party political system. The Democratic–Republicans, the party of Jackson and Van Buren, had become simply the Democratic party. The National Republicans, under the leadership of Henry Clay of Kentucky, took the name of Whigs. In early England, the term originally applied to horse thieves and later meant anyone who opposed the power of the throne. The American Whig party took the name to show their opposition to the tyranny of "King Andrew" Jackson. The Whigs hit the jackpot twice when they put William Henry Harrison (1841) and Millard Fillmore (1850) in the White House. After 1854, however, the party ceased to be a political force. Most of the Whigs joined the newly forming Republican party, which nominated Abraham Lincoln in 1861.

The Whigs had little hope of beating Martin Van Buren outright in the election of 1836. He was the choice of the people's still popular hero, Andrew Jackson. The Whigs themselves did not have a known leader, nor a party platform. They did not even hold a nominating convention. Instead, they hoped to split the Democratic vote so badly that Van Buren would not get a majority in the Electoral College. Therefore, different Whig candidates ran in different parts of the country. For instance,

Daniel Webster ran in New England and William Henry Harrison in the northwest, where he had successfully battled the Indians as a U.S. Army general.

Nice plan, perhaps, but it didn't work. Although Van Buren was not particularly popular, certainly not in the South, he did manage a 170–124 electoral vote count against all combined opponents. His popular majority, however, was small—765,483 against 739,795 for all the Whigs—and his opposition in Congress was large.

And continuing in the grand tradition begun with Jackson's campaign, the mudslinging rolled on! New York's William Seward called Van Buren a "crawling reptile." Even virtuous old J.Q. Adams speculated that Little Van might be "illegitimate." That was about as low a blow as one could deliver at the time.

The Democrats were not above a little name calling themselves. Using the press, they resorted to such petty phrases concerning William Henry Harrison as "the hero of forty defeats" and "a red petticoat general," whatever that meant. Things got so nasty that Little Van took to walking around with two pistols stuck in his belt. He often campaigned as "Old Kinderhook" Van Buren. According to one story, from those initials came the common use of the slang term "OK."

Despite all the mudslinging and general surliness, a surprisingly cheery eighth President of the United States was inaugurated on March 4, 1837. At the age of 54, he had inherited a nation now grown to 26 states. Arkansas and Michigan were admitted in 1836 and 1837, respectively. During his four years in office, the population would surpass 17 million.

Little Van's cheery smile didn't last long, however. He was almost immediately hit with the Panic of 1837. His opponents thought he got what he deserved since the panic, they said, stemmed from Andrew Jackson's anti-U.S. Bank policies. But the depression was harsh and would last for seven years. Aided by a bad wheat crop in 1836, food prices skyrocketed. The price of cotton fell. State banks folded, with a loss of $9 million to the government alone. Rents doubled, people fought in the streets over flour, businesses collapsed, suffering was everywhere.

Van Buren may not have been responsible for the depression, but he didn't do much to ease it either. He adopted a sort of stand-fast-and-let's-see attitude. It wasn't that he was shirking responsibility, The President—and most of the nation—really believed that the less government interfered with the economy, the better. Rather than getting involved with the plight of individual farmers and manufacturers, he felt it was his job to keep the Treasury out of the red and build a sound economy.

Even if this was great policy, Van Buren's "let's wait and see" attitude made him look indecisive. This was made worse by his fence-sitting over the annexation of Texas. The "Texas question" had been an unresolved problem ever since Van Buren took office.

Since 1823, Mexico had encouraged Americans to move into its Texas territory by offering land grants. The plan worked too well. By the early 1830s, there were more Americans than Mexicans living in the east Texas coastal plains. Many settlers from the U.S. had brought slaves with them, which was against Mexican law.

After a revolution in 1832, General Antonio Santa Anna became Mexico's dictator. He was backed by the Americans, who now referred to themselves as Texans, because Santa Anna promised to give them a separate self-ruled state. He did not, of course. In March 1836, at the small

A Texas Declaration of Independence was read in this unadorned structure on March 2, 1836.

village of Washington-on-the-Brazos, the Americans proclaimed the Independent Republic of Texas. Sam Houston became their leader.

The inevitable war was over in six months. Santa Anna won the famous Battle of the Alamo in San Antonio on March 6, 1836. Every American died in the fight, including those famous frontier heroes, Davy Crockett and Jim Bowie. It was a foolhardy military defense, but the stuff of which enduring legends of bravery are made. The following month, Houston and his ragtail army defeated Santa Anna at the Battle of San Jacinto, near the modern city of Houston.

In July 1836, Congress called for a resolution that would recognize the new republic. But President Jackson, nearing the end of his term, hesitated. He saw the problem of Texas as an internal Mexican struggle and didn't think the United States should get involved. But what really made him hesitate was slavery. It was recognized in the Texas constitution. Personally, Jackson didn't see anything wrong with that, but he was afraid the northern states would make a big issue of it in the presidential campaign that fall. And Jackson wanted his hand-picked candidate, Martin Van Buren, to win. So, Jackson did nothing— that is, until after Van Buren was elected. Then he appointed a representative to the government in Houston, which was the same thing as recognizing the new republic.

Now it was 1840 and Van Buren neared reelection. Most Americans in Texas wanted statehood. But slavery was still legal in the republic. Both the retired Andrew Jackson and Texas leader Sam Houston urged statehood. Van Buren hesitated. He was afraid of conflict with the northern states if a new slave state came into the Union. He was afraid of war with Mexico, whose government feared that a new slave state would mean a return of slavery south of the border. What to do? In the end, Van Buren opposed the annexation of Texas, which did not become a state until 1845. Once again, Van Buren was seen as indecisive.

Even so, Van Buren was not an ineffective President. His biggest achievement was the establishment, despite opposition, of an independent treasury department in 1840. It became permanent in 1846. He limited the workday to ten hours in all federal work projects. In 1837, he soothed ruffled British and American feathers after Canada boarded an American steamer in U.S. waters because it was carrying supplies to a Canadian uprising. In 1840, he got Maine and Canadian citizens to sit down and talk about their fight over boundary lines in the northeastern United States. The result was the Webster–Ashburton Treaty of 1842, which settled various boundary disputes.

Even so, Martin Van Buren was seen as wishy-washy. The power he so magically used for others, he seemed unable to wield for himself. He could not seem to face an obstacle square on. The South thought he was proslavery, the North thought he was antislavery. Lots of people blamed him for the depression.

Into this hostile atmosphere marched the election campaign of 1840. If Americans had thought earlier campaigns to be downright dirty, as the saying goes, "you ain't seen nothin' yet."

It all began rather surprisingly on April 14, 1840, in the hallowed halls of Congress. Representative Charles Ogle of Pennsylvania was delivering a speech on money for repairs to the White House—a mere $3,665. Suddenly, he launched a vicious personal attack on the President, which became known as the "Golden Spoon" speech. By the time he was through, Van Buren might as well have walked out the White House door.

These are some of the things Ogle said the President was guilty of: He wore the same perfume as Queen Victoria of England. His knives, forks, and spoons were made of gold and he used green glass finger bowls. He dined like European royalty while "decent Americans" ate "fried meat and gravy." Carpets for the White House had been bought in Europe "of all places."

All this may seem ridiculous, but in 1840 it had an impact. And, in fact, then, as today, appearances very often count for more than truth. Actually Martin Van Buren spent far less on White House living than did Jackson, for instance, and many others. When Andrew Jackson entered the White House, he was not shy about appropriating money for refurbishing. First, he had architect James Hoban finish the front entrance. It was Hoban's last work on the building he had started 30 years before. The completed entrance, known as the North Portico, was finished in 1829. Its massive 50-foot columns brought dignity to the front of the mansion. It was the last major renovation for nearly 75 years. During Jackson's time, the formal East Room, completed in 1818, was finally furnished. Other historic rooms in the mansion, such as the Green Room, the State Dining Room, and the Blue Room, were refurbished as well. He bought a splendid French silver service for guests and handsome china and crystal from France. The White House grounds were not neglected either. Money was spent to spruce them up, including the planting of two magnolia trees in memory of Jackson's wife. They are now known as the Jackson Magnolias. Under his direction, new fences and benches, stables, and a hothouse appeared. An elaborate system of running water was introduced into the White House in 1835.

By contrast, Van Buren, a widower, did little entertaining, and although he enjoyed fine wines and good food, he usually presided only at small, friendly dinner parties. His sons lived with him in the White House and when Abraham married, Angelica Van Buren became her father-in-law's official hostess.

The Democrats tried to counter the Golden Spoon speech, of course, by proving that Van Buren was actually costing the taxpayers less than any other President. But the die was cast, the deed was done. This young, still growing, still forming country tended to look upon intellect as weakness. Somehow, an interest in culture—especially foreign—appeared to be a slap at the rugged, can-do spirit of America.

It was a bad time to be Martin Van Buren and a good time to be William Henry Harrison. Suddenly, this relatively little known military man who had defeated the Shawnee chief Tecumseh at Tippecanoe in 1811 was a hero. He was molded in the likes of Jackson, a champion of the "little people."

The result could not have been worse for Little Van. He was beaten 234 to 60 electoral votes. Even his home state of New York didn't vote for him.

The master politician was not quite ready to give up, however. He returned to Kinderhook and moved into a remodeled mansion that he named Lindenwald. In 1844, then President Tyler offered him a seat on the Supreme Court. Crafty Little Van said no. He was aiming for bigger things—another try for the Democratic nomination. He lost out because of his opposition to Texas entering the Union as a slave state. Even his old friend Andrew Jackson got disgusted with him on that issue and favored candidate James Polk, who took the nomination and the White House.

In the 1848 campaign, Van Buren was a candidate for the Free-Soil party: Free Soil, Free Speech, Free Labor, and Free Men. "Free speech" was actually another term for "antislavery." Party members

A pro-Harrison campaign ribbon extolled the candidate's supposed humble beginnings in a rustic cabin and his victories over the Shawnee Indians at Tippecanoe in 1811 and a force made up of British soldiers and Indian warriors at the Thames River in Ontario in 1813.

were opposed to the "gag rule," which limited debate in the House on the topic of slavery. As a third party candidate, Van Buren faced Lewis Cass of the Democrats and Zachary Taylor of the Whigs. Taylor won and Van Buren quit politics. For a few years, he traveled in Europe, exploring his family's roots. Back home in New York, he was greatly saddened by the outbreak of the Civil War but expressed his complete confidence in President Abraham Lincoln. An asthma sufferer, he died at the age of 78 in Kinderhook, New York, on July 29, 1862.

Historians say that after Andrew Jackson, the White House saw no outstanding leaders until tall and lanky Abraham Lincoln took the oath of office in 1861. It is certainly true that the terms of Presidents Van Buren through Pierce were mostly short and the Presidents themselves largely forgotten. Perhaps the rough, boisterous nation simply overshadowed those who tried to lead it through these formative years.

How ironic that the man who could so skillfully mastermind the campaigns of others was unable to do so for himself. Martin Van Buren always believed that one's political enemy could be a personal friend. For instance, he saw nothing odd about having John C. Calhoun, the man he nudged aside to get to the vice presidency, to the White House for dinner. In turn, of course, those who came for dinner saw nothing wrong with stabbing the President in his political back if it suited their political purposes. In 1828, Van Buren had assured the election of Andrew Jackson by the start of what became known as mudslinging. In the election of 1840, Van Buren's opponents used the master politician's own tactics. Could this elegant little man who enjoys fine wines in the "newly decorated" White House *really* be a Democrat, they asked? Could someone who doesn't eat fried meat and gravy *really* be a man of the people?

The American public thought about it and said no. Master politician Van Buren went down to defeat, giving new meaning to that old adage: Turnabout is fair play.

Names in the News in Van Buren's Time

William Lloyd Garrison (1805–1879):

American abolitionist, born Newburyport, Massachusetts; founded famous antislavery journal, the *Liberator* (1831).

Richard Mentor Johnson (1780–1850):

Kentucky frontiersman, brilliant soldier. Van Buren's running mate (1836); only vice president ever elected by the U.S. Senate—no candidate had received a majority in the Electoral College.

Mary Lyon (1797–1849):

Massachusetts-born pioneer in education for women. Founded Mount Holyoke Seminary (1837) (now Mount Holyoke College), nation's first permanent institution of higher education for women.

Horace Mann (1796–1859):

American educator, revolutionized public school education, established first U.S. normal school (1839); first secretary Massachusetts Board of Education; president Antioch College, Ohio (1852–1859).

An American cartoon, about 1850, titled "Like Meets Like," compares abolitionist William Lloyd Garrison (right) and South Carolina secessionist Laurence Kiett as equal threats to the Union.

Chapter Three

Harrison and the Shortest Term

William Henry Harrison (1841)

*O*n a list of those who made a difference in the White House, William Henry Harrison would have to be last. But how could he have made a difference? He was on the job less than 31 days! At age 68, he was the oldest man up to that time to become President. He was inaugurated on March 4, 1841, came down with pneumonia on March 27, and died on April 4.

Besides having the shortest term, Harrison was the first U.S. President to die in office. His wife, Anna, is in the record books with an unusual "first." She never got to act officially as First Lady. In fact, she never even got to see the White House! She had not yet left her home in Ohio when the news came of her husband's death.

For such a short time on the national scene, Harrison is surprisingly well remembered, if only for the slogan "Tippecanoe and Tyler, too." "Tyler" refers to Harrison's running mate in the election of 1840. "Tippecanoe" is the famous battle that made Harrison a well-known, if perhaps overrated, Indian fighter.

Imagine that it is election time, 1840. You listen to and you believe the Whig's campaign message. That means you believe William Henry Harrison was born in a log cabin and drinks hard cider. You think he is cast in the mold of Davy Crockett and the people's hero, Andrew Jackson. You see him as a bold, roughneck, plow-pushing farmer, in short, the perfect opponent to "dandy" Martin Van Buren.

Well, not exactly. Electioneering has taken you in. The only log cabin Harrison ever had contained five rooms and was built for his bride when he was in the army in Ohio. Once out of service, he built a larger, more suitable home and tucked the cabin into a corner of it.

Harrison was actually born in a three-story brick mansion on the family plantation in Charles City County, Virginia, on February 9, 1773. His wealthy father, Benjamin, had signed the Declaration of Independence. One of seven children, young William graduated from Hampden-Sydney College in Virginia in 1790 and went to medical school. A year later, he changed his mind and joined the army.

Stationed in North Bend, Ohio, in 1795, Lieutenant Harrison met and married Anna Tuthill Symmes, daughter of a well-to-do judge and farmer. They would have ten children. Once out of the army, Harrison became the first congressional representative from the Northwest Territory. He helped to pass a bill that divided this huge parcel of land into two smaller territories—Ohio

Harrison's birthplace in Charles City County, Virginia, later served as a Union hospital for General George B. McClellan's forces during the Northern drive toward Richmond in 1862.

and Indiana. Ohio became a state in 1802, Indiana in 1816. By 1800, Harrison was governor of the Indiana Territory.

Harrison was generally regarded as a genial and fair man, although at times he took both sides of the slavery question. When he dealt with Native Americans, he also sat on both sides of the fence. Given presidential power to negotiate treaties with them, Harrison did so with fair bargaining but also with threats. However, he did protect Native Americans to some extent, for instance, ordering them to be inoculated against smallpox.

In the early 1800s, two Shawnee brothers and chiefs, Tecumseh and Tenskwatawa, were quite successful at uniting other Indian nations in the Northwest Territory against the settlers. In the fall of 1809, Harrison signed a treaty with the Miami tribe that gave more than two million acres of land to the federal government. Tecumseh declared the land was not the Miami's to sell. He warned the new-comers against trespassing.

Although Chief Tecumseh was not present at Tippecanoe in 1811 when forces commanded by Harrison defeated the Shawnees, he was present two years later at the Thames River battle where he was killed.

But in the summer of 1811, Harrison, now commissioned a brigadier general, led his troops into the territory. Tecumseh was away, but Tenskwatawa, called the Prophet, was camped on the Tippecanoe River in what is now northern Indiana. Harrison had orders from President Madison to give the Shawnee the chance to surrender. Against the advice of his aides, he told his men to camp and wait until the next day so he could talk peace.

But in the predawn hours of November 7, 1811, the Shawnee attacked. The battle was short and bloody, and Harrison reported that it was the worst defeat the Indians had ever suffered. Actually, 188 troops were killed and only a few dozen Shawnee. But the Indians were indeed driven off by superior numbers and their abandoned town was burned.

As a military battle, this event didn't accomplish much except to infuriate the Shawnee and send them straight to the side of the British in the War of 1812. But it did make William Henry Harrison, who after all had performed well, the hero of Tippecanoe and provided a lasting campaign slogan.

In the War of 1812 against the British, Harrison was the U.S. commander in the Northwest. He captured the town of Detroit on September 29, 1813, and fought the British on the Thames River in Canada, where Tecumseh was killed.

Harrison spent the next few years in government service. He was a congressman from Ohio (1816–1819), a U.S. senator (1828–1829), and the U.S. minister to Colombia in South America (1828–1829) during the administration of J.Q. Adams.

Back in the United States, Harrison joined the Whig party along with others who were opposed to Andrew Jackson. He was the Whig candidate in the Northwest Territory against Martin Van Buren in 1836. Although Van Buren won, quiet, affable Harrison had proved to be surprisingly good at getting votes, even in a losing cause. This was a fact the Whigs did not forget. When the 1840 election rolled around, Harrison was their man.

The election of 1840 reached a new low in American campaign tactics. While the Whigs accused the incumbent President of outrageous spending in the White House, the Democrats belittled Harrison's military leadership. They called him Granny, because he was 67 years old at the time, and General Mum, because he never said anything important while campaigning. They also declared that it was Van Buren's running mate, Richard M. Johnson, who was the real hero, not Harrison. Johnson, they claimed, serving under Harrison in the War of 1812, was the man who shot Chief Tecumseh.

Besides the mudslinging, the election of 1840 goes down as the first musical campaign in U.S. history. It is said that notes, not votes, got Harrison into the White House. Every American man, woman, and child marched around the country with such ditties as this on their lips:

> *The beautiful girls, God bless their souls,*
> > *souls, souls, the country through.*
> *Will all, to a man, do all they can*
> > *For Tippecanoe and Tyler, too.*

Or this little slap against Van Buren:

> *When Martin was housed like a chattel,*
> *Opposed to the war as you know,*
> *Our hero was foremost in battle,*
> *And conquered at Tippecanoe.*

It may not have been "Yankee Doodle Dandy," but poor Martin Van Buren didn't have a chance against such a musical onslaught. The hero of Tippecanoe won big. The electoral vote count was 234 to 60! The popular vote favored "Granny" Harrison by almost 150,000!

Alas, for William Henry Harrison, he was elected President of the United States. At age 68, he took the office already worn out from campaigning and endless speechmaking. By Inauguration Day, his arm was sore and swollen from all that hand shaking. But more than anything else, it was probably his friendly nature that did him in. Inauguration Day—March 4, 1841—dawned cold and bitter in Washington, D.C. Many people had worked hard for Harrison's election. Now they stood around the steps of the Capitol building waiting for his speech. The new President could not disappoint them, and so he spoke for nearly two hours. It was not a wise decision.

Harrison got no rest during the next few weeks either. Except for aides and staff, he was alone in the White House. Anna Harrison was unable to make the inauguration due to illness but was scheduled to arrive shortly. And once again, the President's own nature plagued him. A generous man, eager to please his friends, he promised a job in his new administration to almost anyone who asked. Sometimes he promised two or three differ-ent people the same job! The result was chaos at the White House. One visitor said that anyone who walked through the front door got either the promise of a job, a loan of money, or a free meal.

Harrison was tired. First, he caught a cold. By March 27, the doctors detected pneumonia. He grew worse and became deliri-ous, at one point saying, "I cannot bear this. Don't trouble me."

On April 4, 1841, a month after taking office, the ninth President of the United States was dead. The news reached his wife as she was about to leave to assume her duties as First Lady. The funeral, according to the press, "was magnificent" and "bet-ter arranged" than the inauguration.

President Harrison's funeral set the pattern for all such future ceremonies. Black drapes covered the mirrors and paint-ings inside the White House and black banners draped the

On his death bed, President Harrison was attended by his niece and nephew to the right, a Protestant minister (to the left of the bed) and a physician, and Daniel Webster, secretary of state, to the left at the foot of the bed.

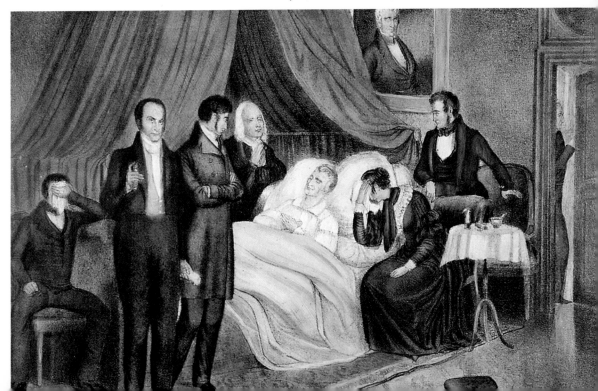

exterior. The coffin was placed in the entrance hall so that the public could file through. Thousands of people lined the streets as six white horses led the funeral procession through the city.

It was a shock to the young nation to have a President die in office, especially after so short a time. Many citizens wore black armbands or carried special mourning ribbons. The old hero of Tippecanoe was finally laid to rest in North Bend, Ohio, with respectful goodbyes from a country that barely knew him.

Names in the News in Harrison's Time

Nathaniel Currier (1813–1888):

Massachusetts-born lithographer; set up business in New York c.1834. With partner J. Merritt Ives (1824–1895) depicted manners and events in American life, including the death of President Harrison showing mourners around his bed.

Tecumseh (c.1768–1813):

Chief of the Shawnee tribe; with brother, Tenskwatawa (defeated at Battle of Tippecanoe), united western tribes against settlers. Sided with British in War of 1812; killed at Battle of Thames (October 5, 1813).

Chapter Four

Gentlemanly John Tyler

John Tyler (1841-1845)

*I*f the country was shocked about the death of William Henry Harrison after 31 days in office, imagine how Vice President Tyler felt! There he stood at the front door of his home in Williamsburg, Virginia, having been rudely awakened by a messenger's loud knocking. It was barely sunrise on April 5, 1841. The messenger was Fletcher Webster, son of Secretary of State Daniel Webster. Acting as his father's chief courier, Fletcher had been riding horseback all night to deliver the news that the President was dead. The vice president didn't even know Harrison was ill!

It is difficult for twentieth-century Americans to understand travel and communication in the first half of the nineteenth century. There was no instant news at all. There were no telephones or radios. Samuel Morse would not set up the first U.S. telegraph line until 1844. Except for horse or boat, travel to spread news was very limited. The first U.S. railroad—the Baltimore and Ohio—did not appear until 1830. The first U.S. automobile wouldn't be built for another 63 years! In terms of quick communication in 1841, Williamsburg, Virginia, which is less than 200 miles from Washington, D.C., might as well have been on the moon.

No one knows how Tyler reacted to the courier's news, but surely he was stunned. Today, the office of vice president is often the butt of political jokes: it's boring, there's nothing to do, it's a going-nowhere position. But twentieth-century vice presidents at least have an official home. They live in a lovely old house on the U.S. Naval Observatory grounds in Washington, D.C. They even have an official job, sometimes. They preside over the Senate and vote in case of a tie. And most modern Presidents at least try to give the impression that they are keeping their vice presidents informed on everything "just in case."

This was definitely not so in earlier times. From Adams to Tyler, vice presidents after Inauguration Day generally packed up and went home, to Williamsburg or Massachusetts or wherever they lived. They just went on with what they were doing before the campaign. They had no official place, no official duties. The country more or less forgot about them. A vice president just didn't become President unless he ran on his own and was elected. It didn't happen, until Tyler.

Not only had it happened to tall and skinny, gentlemanly John Tyler, but now what? Was he actually the President? Or was he only the acting President? What had the Founding Fathers meant when they included this succession clause in the Constitution:

In Case of the Removal of the President
from Office, or of his Death, Resignation,
or Inability to discharge the Powers and
Duties of the said Office, the Same shall
devolve on the Vice President...

Did this mean that the Powers and Duties went to the individual who was the vice president or to the *office* of the vice president? Strange as it may seem today, no one was sure back in 1841. And there was no one to ask. The last surviving person who had helped to frame the Constitution was James Madison, and he had died five years earlier. Modern historians don't all agree on this point either, but many feel that the Founding Fathers meant that the vice president should become acting President only until the next election. In any case, as of February 10, 1967, the uncertainty has been cleared up by the Twenty-Fifth Amendment to the

U.S. Constitution. This clearly states in part: "In case of the removal of the President from office or of his death or resignation, the Vice President shall become President."

Back in 1841, John Tyler took the matter into his own hands. He had no intention of being an acting President, and he didn't much like the new nickname his opponents had quickly given him: "His Accidency." Once he got the news from Fletcher Webster, the two of them had breakfast and returned to Washington by river steamboat, a trip of 21 hours. At the Indian Queen Hotel in the capital, a little more than two days after Harrison's death, John Tyler had himself sworn in as the tenth President of the United States. Thus he became the first U.S. vice president to take office on the death of a President. He was also, up until that time, the youngest President: 51 years old. As a third distinction, he still holds the record as the President with the most children: 14.

If for no other reason, by his act of taking the oath of office, John Tyler made an impact on the White House. Tyler himself did not believe it was necessary for him to take the oath. He thought that Harrison's death *automatically* made him President. But since no one was sure, he was sworn in. Since that time, eight vice presidents have taken the oath on the death or resignation of a President. The two most recent were Lyndon Johnson after John Kennedy's assassination in 1963 and Gerald Ford after Richard Nixon's resignation in 1974.

If Tyler was surprised at being in the White House, political Washington was stunned! John Quincy Adams wrote in his diary that no one had ever even considered Tyler as President. Who *was* this man?

For one thing, he was a Virginian, the sixth President from that state. He was born, like Harrison, in Charles City County, on March 29, 1790. His parents were John, a judge, and Mary Armistead Tyler. One of eight children, he graduated from William and Mary College in 1807 and was practicing law by the age of 21.

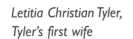

Letitia Christian Tyler,
Tyler's first wife

Tyler grew into a tall man with sharp features and a long nose. He was graceful and charming with a gentlemanly demeanor that sometimes covered up a good dose of stubbornness. In 1813, he married Letitia Christian and by all accounts had a happy 27-year marriage, which included seven children. Four of them would accompany him and his wife, confined to a wheelchair, to the White House.

Tyler became a U.S. senator in 1827 but resigned in 1836 over a dispute with his state's legislature, even though his name was brought up by the Whigs for vice president.

He decided to run for the Senate again in 1839. When the Whigs were looking around for someone to balance the ticket with Harrison, they settled—without much enthusiasm—on John Tyler.

President Tyler was in trouble with the Cabinet right from the start. It was, of course, Harrison's Cabinet, led by Secretary of State Daniel Webster. The secretary gently informed the new President that during Harrison's short administration, all decisions had been made democratically, everyone having one vote, including the President. The new President courteously informed the secretary that times had changed. The Cabinet could stay or resign, but the President would lead.

This did not sit well with either the Cabinet or with Henry Clay. What followed was probably inevitable. A Clay-dominated Congress passed bill after bill that favored the federal government. Tyler vetoed ten of them, including two that would have reestablished a national bank. He soon became known as "Old Veto." He also had the dubious honor of being the first President to have a veto overturned by Congress. According to the Constitution, it takes a two-thirds majority in both the House and Senate to override a presidential veto.

About five months after he became President, John Tyler was not winning any popularity contests. There were threats on his life and some members of Congress called for impeachment! On September 14, 1841, his entire Cabinet resigned, with the exception of Daniel Webster, who stood by him.

Strangely enough, in early 1844, the country came close to losing two Presidents within a four-year period. On February 28, Tyler and some 350 guests were aboard the frigate *Princeton* cruising the Potomac River. Tyler's first wife, Letitia, had died two years earlier, and he was now engaged to Julia Gardiner of New York, a wealthy and vivacious woman in her twenties. Julia and her father were among the President's guests. So was Secretary of the Navy Thomas W. Gilmer. The purpose of the cruise was to show off the frigate's new gun, called the Peacemaker. Unfortunately, during the test, the weapon didn't live up to its name. It exploded and killed eight men. In the ensuing panic, both Tyler and Julia Gardiner were pitched into the

Potomac but were rescued. They were married in June 1844, during his last year in the White House. The wedding took place in New York City on dry land.

With all the political and personal woes that confronted John Tyler as President, it is a wonder he accomplished anything at all. Yet he did have some success. The Preemption Act was passed in 1841. It encouraged settlement in western states by offering 160 acres at a minimum payment of $1.25 per acre after 14 months of residence. It was largely superseded by the Homestead Act of 1862, which offered 160 acres for a small fee after five years of residence, or $1.25 an acre after six months.

Julia Gardiner Tyler, Tyler's second wife

Tyler had some success in foreign matters, too. He signed a commerce treaty with China and declared the Hawaiian Islands to be covered by the Monroe Doctrine, the declaration issued by President Monroe that the American continents were no longer open to European colonization.

As the election of 1844 drew closer, Tyler knew he had little chance of winning a term on his own. The Whigs would not nominate him, and the opposition Democrats had won a majority in Congress during the midterm elections. If he couldn't be President again, at least he wanted to do something noteworthy by which he would be remembered. So he settled on Texas.

The idea of making Texas a state had been brewing in Congress for some time. According to popular thinking, the territory was so huge that it might be divided into at least four states. The stumbling block was a familiar one—what about slavery?

Tyler took a familiar route. Leave the slavery issue alone. Texas was important geographically and commercially to the United States. The slavery problem would work out by itself. Daniel Webster disagreed and resigned from the Cabinet, although remaining friendly to Tyler. The President appointed Abel P. Upshur, fellow Virginian, as secretary of state, and they began to work on a secret treaty with the president of Texas, Sam Houston. But before completion, Upshur was killed in an accident.

Word circulated that proslavery John C. Calhoun would take Upshur's job. It wasn't true, but Tyler was afraid to say so for fear of alienating the South. The damage was done. Slavery was back in the news. On June 8, the Senate turned down the annexation of Texas.

By this time, the Democratic party had nominated James Knox Polk for the 1844 fall campaign, the Whigs named Henry Clay, and the Tyler party, made up of conservative Democrats and some Whigs, chose the President. Frightened that Tyler's group would take away votes and cost them the election, the

President Anson Jones declares the end of the Republic of Texas and strikes the Lone Star flag on February 19, 1846, nearly two months after the U.S. Congress had approved of statehood on December 29, 1845.

Democrats gave in on Texas. Tyler and his splinter party supported Polk, who beat Clay in November.

John Tyler finally got his appointment with history. It happened on March 1, 1845, two days before Florida became the twenty-seventh state and three days before he left office. Tyler signed a Senate bill approving the admission of Texas. It became the twenty-eighth state in the Union during Polk's administration. With Polk in the White House, Tyler and his young bride moved to a Virginia plantation where he farmed and helped to raise a new set of seven children. He died on January 18, 1862, after suffering a stroke. The tenth President is buried in Richmond, beside the grave of the fifth President, James Monroe.

Pushed unexpectedly into the spotlight, John Tyler spent his presidential years in rather lonely isolation. An honest man who took his duties seriously, he had neither the fighting personality nor the popularity of Andrew Jackson to carry him through. Faced with a hostile Congress and an uncooperative Cabinet, Tyler sat almost powerless in the seat of power—a President without a party.

Names in the News in Tyler's Time

Sam Houston (1793–1863):

Virginia-born soldier, political leader. After Battle of the Alamo, defeated Santa Anna at San Jacinto (1836). President Texas Republic (1836–1838, 1841–1844); U.S. senator (1846–1859); governor of Texas (1859–1861); deposed for refusing allegiance to the Confederacy.

Samuel Finley Breese Morse (1791–1872):

Massachusetts-born inventor. During Tyler administration, Congress appropriated $30,000 for his experimental telegraph line between Washington and Baltimore. On May 24, 1844, sent first message: "What hath God wrought!" His statue stands in Central Park, New York City.

Daniel Webster (1782–1852):

New Hampshire-born statesman, lawyer, senator. Secretary of state under Harrison and Tyler (1841–1843, 1850–1852). Unsuccessful Whig candidate for presidency (1852).

A contemporary cartoon of 1842 shows a tipsy Daniel Webster, right, dining with a smug-looking lion, representing Lord Ashburton, during negotiations for the Webster-Ashburton Treaty which settled the northern border between Canada and the states of Maine and New Hampshire.

Chapter Five

That Dark Horse Polk

James K. Polk (1845-1849)

"*W*ho is this James K. Polk?" scoffed the opposition Whigs during the election campaign of 1844. Some members of his own party weren't even sure. During their convention, the Democrats could not decide on a candidate. Out of the deadlock—and into the White House—ran James Knox Polk, the first dark horse in American presidential politics.

In political terms, a dark horse is an unknown or little known individual who unexpectedly pops out of the pack to win the race. That certainly fit Polk. Although he was familiar to Washington leaders—he'd been in the House of Representatives for 14 years and was governor of Tennessee before that—the American people knew him hardly at all. What the public got as a candidate was a thin, somber, stern-looking man with dignified manners and penetrating eyes. What the public got as a President was a leader of good judgment, iron will, and a strong sense of duty.

Dark horse he may have been, but rarely has a chief executive entered office so in tune with the desires of the people. By the 1840s, the formative years of the United States were in full swing. Confident of their country, Americans were also growing confident of its superiority. In short, they were beginning to believe their own press! All their causes, they believed, were just and all their actions on a high moral ground. Expansion of

In this cartoonlike illustration the explorer John C. Fremont is shown hoisting the American flag on the highest peak of the Rocky Mountains. Mexican officials were highly suspicious of Fremont's expeditions to California and Oregon.

U.S. boundaries became a crusade. Poet Walt Whitman wrote that U.S. expansion was "for the interest of mankind." Newspaperman John L. Sullivan of New York put it more memorably. He declared that it was the "manifest destiny" of the United States "to occupy and to possess the whole of the Continent which Providence has given us."

Into this fervor of a nation caught up in the rapture of its own being stepped James Knox Polk. There could not have been a better match. What was America's "manifest destiny" became his. The will of the people became his will. Polk announced four goals for his administration: he would reduce tariffs, he would establish an independent treasury department (Congress had approved the independent treasury under Van Buren, but it would not be established until Polk's term), and—what the citizens wanted to hear—he would settle the Oregon boundary and acquire California! Manifest destiny, indeed!

The body of the new President was frail. Although he was only 49 years old, he looked far older. The youngest yet in the White House, he would live just three months past his one and only term. What was not frail, however, was his determination or singleness of purpose. The dark horse did just what he said he would do during his four years in office. In the process, he added about a million square miles of land to the expansion-starved country, and three more states joined the Union: Texas (1845), Iowa (1846), and Wisconsin (1848), bringing the total to 30. By the time he retired to Tennessee, no one had to ask, "Who is this James K. Polk?"

He was the first President from the state of North Carolina, where he was born in Mecklenburg County on November 2, 1795. James was the oldest of ten children born to Samuel, a wealthy farmer, and Jane, a staunch Presbyterian. His father did not much agree with his wife's religious beliefs and had a fight with the minister after his son's birth. As a result, Polk was not baptized until he was 54 years old and on his deathbed.

The family moved to Tennessee when James was 11 years old. A sickly boy, James had his gallbladder removed when he was 17. If his body was frail, his will wasn't. It is said the operation was performed without anesthesia.

Polk—a math and classics scholar—graduated with honors from the University of North Carolina in 1818 and headed back to Tennessee. He studied law and was admitted to the bar in 1820. By that time, he had become friendly with his father's old acquaintance, Andrew Jackson. When Jackson ran for President in the election of 1824, Polk, who had spent two years in the Tennessee legislature, ran for the U.S. House of Representatives. Jackson lost, but Polk won and in 1825 took the stagecoach to Washington. Once in the nation's capital, Polk immediately got down to serious work. His colleagues admired his work ethic but were more often than not irritated by his formal manner.

Polk's career in Washington picked up when his old friend Andrew Jackson became President, and it flourished under Martin Van Buren. Polk supported Jackson's attack on the Bank of the United States and colleagues took to calling him "Young Hickory." By 1835, he was Speaker of the House of Representatives. This made him a fair target for anyone who opposed Jackson but didn't want to go on record as saying so. Representative Henry A. Wise once got so angry at Polk that he called him a "little petty tyrant." Dueling was still in fashion, and Wise hoped to incur Polk's wrath. It didn't work. Polk remained steady as always.

In 1839, a reluctant Polk was elected governor of Tennessee. He really wanted to remain in Washington but felt he had to accept his party's choice.

Then came the election of 1844. Henry Clay, on the Whig ticket, didn't care who his opponent was. With incumbent President Tyler on everyone's hate list, it looked like it might be Van Buren for the Democrats. Polk's name came up as vice president because of his long service to the Jacksonians.

But as they might say in politics, you never know.

As the nominating conventions neared, neither Clay nor Van Buren seemed to read the expansion fever in the country. Because of the slavery problem, they both decided to avoid the issue of annexing Texas—a fatal mistake. It was a mistake, however, recognized by that crafty old politician now retired at the Hermitage in Tennessee. Andrew Jackson was still a powerful force in the party. He told Democratic leaders that Van Buren could never win with his stand on Texas, and neither would Clay. America wanted to expand. So did Polk.

The Democrats met in Baltimore to decide on a nominee. With Jackson's advice in mind, his followers deadlocked the convention—meaning that no one had a majority of votes—until the ninth ballot. Dark horse James Knox Polk emerged the surprise choice.

Polk was aided in his campaign, not so much by discussion of important issues—the candidates talked little about those—but by slogans. The public was soon awash in quips and sprightly sayings. "All of Oregon, all of Texas!" "All of Oregon or none!" And the catchiest of all: "Fifty-four forty or Fight!" This, of course, referred to the Oregon boundary question, meaning that the United States wanted all of the Oregon territory north to the latitude of 54 degrees 40 minutes.

It was a close race. Polk may have been for expansion, but Henry Clay was a very popular and well-known national figure. Polk won 170 to 105 in the Electoral College, but with less than

40,000 popular votes. His vice president was George M. Dallas of Philadelphia.

When the eleventh President came to Washington, so did a First Lady who certainly brought a startling change to the White House! She was Sarah Childress Polk, who had married the President in 1824. Sarah Polk was as serious as her husband. She was also a staunch and strong-willed Calvinist. If Washington leaders were looking forward to a new social order, they got a bit more than they bargained for. From now on, said the First Lady, there would be no wine, no dancing, and no card games in the White House! Not only would there be no wine at public receptions, there would be no refreshments at all! It is said that the Polk years would have been unbearably

Sarah Childress Polk

dull had not party-loving Dolley Madison, now in her eighties, still lived in the nation's capital. She continued to drink, take snuff, and play cards at her lively receptions.

In fairness to Sarah Polk, however, she was just as hard-working as her husband. Like him, she had little taste for "time unprofitably spent." When it was clear near the end of his term that the President's health was failing, she became his confidential secretary and did a highly competent job in trying to lighten his workload.

Soon after moving into the White House, Polk, true to his campaign promise, tackled the prickly issue of Oregon. Great Britain and the United States had a long-running dispute over this territory. The English claimed it based on explorations of Sir Francis Drake back in 1579. The Americans claimed it dating from Captain Robert Gray's discovery of the mouth of the Columbia River in 1792.

Even though Polk had campaigned on the "fifty-four forty" line, the President told James Buchanan, his secretary of state, to offer the forty-ninth parallel as the boundary. This would just

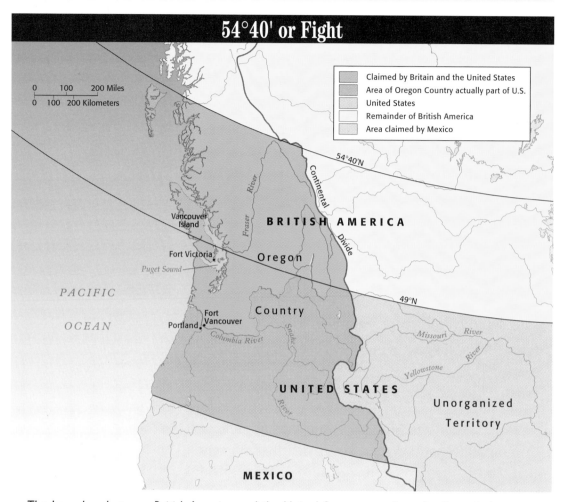

54°40' or Fight

Legend:
- Claimed by Britain and the United States
- Area of Oregon Country actually part of U.S.
- United States
- Remainder of British America
- Area claimed by Mexico

The boundary between British America and the United States runs along the forty-ninth parallel to Puget Sound, then dips south around Vancouver Island.

extend the northern U.S. border in a straight line to the Pacific. The British said no. They would take the forty-ninth parallel, but only to the mouth of the Columbia. This would leave them in control of the northwest Oregon fur trade and the excellent harbor of Puget Sound. A surprisingly tough President Polk wrote in his diary that "the only way to treat John Bull [nickname for a typical Englishman] is to look him straight in the eye." Polk and the Congress stood firm and took a gamble on war, even though trouble with Mexico was looming.

But Great Britain wanted war no more than did the Americans and certainly not over land so far from home. Besides, by now most of the settlers in the territory were Americans anyway. The treaty was signed on June 15, 1846. Check off one of Polk's four campaign promises.

American settlers had been flocking to the Oregon Territory since the 1830s, and by the 1840s, deep wagon ruts marked what became known as the Oregon Trail. With the boundary settled, ever more pioneers trekked west to Oregon's glorious and fertile Willamette Valley. It was a rough go of some 2,000 miles for the so-called prairie schooners, the durable if uncomfortable canvas-covered Conestoga wagons.

The jumping-off point for the Oregon Trail was Independence, Missouri. There, the wagons gathered, and with captain and experienced guide, traveled along the Missouri River to the Platte River and into the future state of Kansas. From there, the settlers were really on their own, in territory claimed by Native

Drawn by William Henry Jackson, this illustration shows a wagon train on the Oregon Trail alongside the Sweetwater River at Devil's Gate in Wyoming.

Americans and without U.S. government protection. Each night the 100 or so wagons would pull into a circle and post guards to protect them against wild animals and keep their own animals enclosed. When a wagon train hit southern Wyoming and made it through the South Pass over the Rockies, it faced hundreds of miles along the twisting Snake River, through arid stretches with little grass for cattle and little fresh water for anyone. Only the heartiest made it to the Willamette Valley below the Columbia River, and never as many as had started out.

One of the most remarkable of all westward migrations occurred in 1847, during Polk's administration. The Mormon religion, known formally as the Church of Jesus Christ of the Latterday Saints, was founded by Joseph Smith, Jr., of Palmyra, New York, in 1830. Claiming to be God's prophet, Smith asserted that angels had led him to a book of God's revelations written on gold plates, which he translated into the *Book of Mormon.*

This new religion did not fit in well with other Christian denominations. The Mormons kept a closely knit type of social life and some practiced polygamy, meaning a man could have more than one wife. This practice was followed in the mid-1800's but was outlawed by the Mormons in 1890. Antagonism from their neighbors because of their beliefs kept the Mormons on the move until they ended up in Illinois in 1839. Antagonism also turned to violence against Smith, which brought about his murder by a mob.

Brigham Young, brilliant and strong-willed, became the new leader. Born in Vermont in 1801, he vowed to lead the Mormons to "the midst of the Rocky Mountains...where we can...build a city in a day and have a government of our own." So began the remarkable journey that took several thousand Mormons from Council Bluffs, Iowa, to Salt Lake City, Utah. They have indeed built themselves a city and a way of life—with many modern changes—that flourishes today. Pioneers' Day, July 24, is a legal holiday in Utah, marking the arrival of Young and the Mormons.

Americans forged many trails to the West during those early years. Probably the most famous was the Santa Fe Trail. Beginning in the early 1820s, merchants had trekked from Independence, Missouri, on a long, lonely, and dangerous journey southwest through Comanche and Osage country. They were headed for Santa Fe, the capital of, and only town in, New Mexico territory, where they traded goods for furs and silver. But early in Polk's administration, Texas became part of the Union. This so angered the Mexicans that they banned Americans from Santa Fe. By then, however, other routes had opened up and westward expansion moved on. After the Oregon settlement, the eyes of the nation turned to California, and another of the President's campaign promises. By the time the Oregon treaty was signed on June 15, 1846, the war with Mexico had already begun. It had been inevitable. The United States was awash in expansion fever, and lush, rich, beautiful California, lining the Pacific shores, was the grand prize. Of course, the grand prize just happened to belong to Mexico.

In late 1845, Polk sent John Slidell, a Louisiana Democrat, as his representative to Mexico with an offer: as much as $30 million for California and New Mexico, with the Rio Grande River as the boundary for the state of Texas. The Mexican government wouldn't even see Slidell.

Shortly thereafter, in April 1846, fighting began in a disputed area of southern Texas between the Nueces River and the Rio Grande. Polk had sent General Zachary Taylor, who would succeed him as President, into the area to protect the border. Taylor claimed the Mexicans had attacked, giving Polk a reason to declare war, which Congress did on May 13, 1846.

Polk hoped to win the war by doing more talking than fighting. But he felt that Mexico would not listen without an offer of money. He asked Congress for $2 million. However, David Wilmot, Democratic congressman from Pennsylvania, attached a condition to the bill: slavery must be excluded from any land acquired from Mexico. The Wilmot Proviso wasn't approved by the generally proslavery Senate, and neither was the money. Just part of the continuing controversy over slavery, the Wilmot Proviso was introduced several more times as well, and voted down each time. Polk would have vetoed it anyway.

To Polk, this meant California and New Mexico would have to be fought for, not negotiated. That proved rather easy. An army led by Colonel Stephen W. Kearny marched from Kansas to the Pacific, meeting only scant resistance near San Diego and Los Angeles. By January 1847, California and New Mexico were part of the United States. Chalk off Polk's second campaign promise.

But the war was still on. Zachary Taylor, in defeating the Mexicans in Texas, had become a national hero. He was victorious at the battle of Monterrey in Mexico on September 1846. The following February, he defeated General Santa Anna in a bloody battle at Buena Vista. But Polk chose General Winfield Scott to lead the U.S. Army into Mexico. In a brilliant campaign, Scott invaded Mexico by sea, won the battle of Veracruz in March, and reached Mexico City in September 1847. Santa Anna's government collapsed and the war was over.

With the Treaty of Guadalupe Hidalgo on February 19, 1848, Polk and the country had what they wanted. California and New Mexico were part of the United States, the Rio Grande became the Texas border, and Mexico settled for $15 million for Texas north of the Rio Grande, New Mexico, and upper California—much less than the Americans offered back in 1845. Besides the enormous acquisition of new land, the United States

The flag of the California Republic was first raised in June 1846 when settlers took over Sonoma. Two years later California became part of the United States when Mexico ceded the area at the end of the Mexican War.

now had important new outlets for trade on the Pacific coast. And in his last message to Congress in December 1848, Polk announced that gold had been discovered in the *American territory* of California! Manifest destiny indeed!

With the Treaty of Guadalupe Hidalgo, Polk had completed his campaign promises to the American people—something of a milestone itself in American politics. Two years earlier, the Independent Treasury Act, which had been repealed by the Whigs in 1840, was restored. It made the U.S. Treasury completely independent of the banking and financial system of the nation. Also under Polk, the Walker Tariff was enacted. It greatly reduced taxes on imports set by the Whigs in 1842.

Polk's devotion to duty wore him out. Although his record was rather remarkable, he received little recognition for it. By the time he and his wife headed for retirement in Tennessee, his hair had turned gray and he walked with a slow and halting step. The ex-President was an old man at age 54. Plagued throughout his life by health problems, he died on June 15, 1849, only a few months after he left the White House. He is buried in Nashville, Tennessee.

Polk had proved to be a man of his word, which is perhaps enough to have earned him a place in history. Today, he is generally regarded as a man of integrity who would not be bluffed or bullied. He had ability and the strength to carry out what he saw as his duty. An excellent administrator, he was a tireless worker. In a group not noted for strong leadership, he is, however, often recognized as the strongest President between Jackson and Lincoln. In directing the war with Mexico, he was the first U.S. President actually to fulfill the title that all Presidents have: Commander in Chief of U.S. military forces. Said one historian of the eleventh President: "His mind was rigid, narrow, and obstinate...but if it was narrow it was also powerful, and he had guts."

Names in the News in Polk's Time

Christopher "Kit" Carson (1809–1868):

Kentucky-born scout and trapper; guide for Fremont's California expeditions (1842, 1843, 1845); fought with Kearny in battle for California; served in Southwest during Civil War.

George M. Dallas (1792–1864):

Philadelphia-born, Princeton-educated; second choice for Polk's running mate. Championed annexation of Texas with slogan: "Polk, Dallas, and Texas." Texas remembered his support and named a county after him.

John C. Fremont (1813–1890):

Georgia-born explorer, army officer, known as "the pathfinder." Explored Mississippi and Missouri Rivers; mapped Oregon Trail; led California expeditions. Fought in battle for California during war with Mexico. Republican party nominee (1856), defeated by Buchanan. Retired as major general (1890).

Washington Irving (1783–1859):

New York-born author, lawyer. Minister to Spain during Polk's first year in office. Most famous as author of *Rip Van Winkle* and *The Legend of Sleepy Hollow*.

Walt Whitman (1819–1892):

New York-born poet; editor for Brooklyn *Eagle* (1846–1848), where he became caught up in American "expansion fever"; published famous book of verse *Leaves of Grass* (1855), which was denounced by reviewers. Among most famous works are poems dedicated to Lincoln, including *O Captain! My Captain!*

This whimsical cartoon of Walt Whitman was drawn by Max Beerbohm in 1904.

Chapter Six

Old Rough-and-Ready Taylor

Zachary Taylor (1849-1850)

America loves its war heroes. Maybe it began in 1776 when Washington crossed the Delaware and caught the British by surprise at Trenton, New Jersey. Sometimes, being a war hero has meant a ticket to the White House. That was true for Andrew Jackson after New Orleans, for U.S. Grant after the Civil War, for Teddy Roosevelt after the Spanish-American War, and for Dwight Eisenhower after World War II. It was also true for General Zachary Taylor, whose exploits during the Mexican War (1846–1848) paved his way to the White House as the twelfth President of the United States.

Taylor earned the nickname "Old Rough and Ready," another catchy campaign slogan. He was brave, outspoken, and a self-made soldier who commanded a rough, wild band of Texas volunteers. Mainly hardfisted cowboys, they went into battle with an eerie cry straight off the cattle range. That same strange sound struck terror in the hearts of Northern soldiers during the Civil War when they heard the "rebel yell." Although Taylor led his men to victory over Mexico, he was not considered a brilliant military man, being somewhat over-cautious and short on strategy.

A national hero and popular President, Old Rough and Ready looked like his nickname. He had a rather strange body. His head was large, his face craggy, and his legs too short for his torso. He liked to wear a farmer's wide-brimmed straw hat, giving him an almost comical appearance. He was anything but. And actually, he was not rough and ready in the White House, surviving only one year and 127 days in office.

His nickname did not fit his background either. Taylor came from Virginia aristocracy, the seventh President from that state. His father, Richard, descended from a long line of wealthy planters and was a lieutenant colonel in the American Revolution. His mother, Sarah Dabney Strother Taylor, had been educated by European tutors. Zachary was born in Orange County, Virginia, on November 24, 1784, the third son in a family of nine children. Soon after his birth, the family settled down to farm near Louisville, Kentucky. Although the Taylors tutored their children, Zachary's formal education was limited, mostly obtained from wandering schoolteachers.

At the age of 23, Taylor joined the army as a first lieutenant. Except for a brief period, he remained in the military for 40 years and rose to the rank of major general. He married Margaret Mackall Smith in 1810. Of their six children, four survived to adulthood.

By 1844, Taylor was a brigadier general and commanding officer at Fort Jesup, Louisiana. For years he had traveled about the country on military duty, He gained a reputation as a courageous leader who had a good relationship with his men and was a fair administrator concerning Native Americans.

Taylor wound up in Louisiana because trouble was brewing. Mexico was still unhappy over the annexation of Texas and dissatisfied with the Rio Grande as the boundary line. Taylor was sent to the Rio Grande with 4,000 men. Fighting broke out on April 25, 1846, but

Margaret Smith Taylor

by the time Congress declared war on May 13, Taylor and his out-numbered army had been victorious at Palo Alto and Resaca de la Palma.

Old Rough and Ready was an instant national hero and celebrity. The Whigs were calling for him as President. He was even more of a hero after winning a bloody battle at Monterrey. However, it was there that his overcautious nature showed up. Although the victor, Taylor knew that it would take time and effort to clear all the Mexicans from their defensive positions in the city. Reasoning that President Polk was anxious to talk peace, Taylor let the Mexicans walk out of town with their firepower.

Polk said Taylor had muffed a chance to end the war. The President wasn't too happy with the general's growing popularity anyway. The main responsibility for conducting the war was turned over to General Winfield Scott, known as Old Fuss and Feathers for his vain and pompous manner. In later years, Scott did not look back kindly upon his old rival. He said: "General Taylor's mind has not been enlarged and refreshed by reading, or much converse with the world." He did soften that a bit, however, adding that Taylor had "pure, uncorrupted morals, combined with indomitable courage."

If Polk thought Scott's promotion put Taylor out to pasture, he was wrong. Mexican general Santa Anna heard that Old Rough and Ready had been ordered to remain in Monterrey

General Zachary Taylor, mounted on the white horse, directed American troops at the Battle of Buena Vista, a ranch near Monterrey, Mexico, February 22–23, 1847.

and instructed to conduct only defensive operations. He also heard that many of Taylor's troops had been transferred to Scott's command. All of this was true. Figuring on an easy victory, Santa Anna marched an overwhelming force toward Monterrey.

Santa Anna had committed a cardinal sin of war: Never underestimate the enemy. Taylor simply disobeyed orders. With about one-quarter the number of Santa Anna's troops, he left Monterrey and camped his men to the southwest at a ranch called Buena Vista. For two days the badly outnumbered Americans fought the Mexicans to a standstill. Santa Anna retreated. Taylor was a bigger hero than ever.

Despite the general's popularity, his election was not a shoo-in for the Whigs. For one thing, Taylor wasn't really sure about running. He knew he had little experience with matters of state, and besides, his wife wasn't so certain the White House would be good for his health. On that point, she was certainly correct.

Although inexperienced, Taylor was not naive. He held himself somewhat apart from politics and managed to stay in the middle on practically all issues. The Whigs had to convince him to declare himself one of them about six weeks before the election. Fortunately for the general, he was helped by the opposition. The Democrats nominated Senator Lewis Cass of Michigan, which annoyed the Free-Soilers (see page 35), who wanted slavery prohibited in the western territories. They in turn nominated former President Martin Van Buren. That effectively split the opposition and helped the 64-year-old Taylor into the White House. He won by 163 electoral votes to 127 for Cass and none for Van Buren. Taylor's running mate was Millard Fillmore of New York.

Once in the White House, Taylor's inexperience brought him grief. He had trouble picking Cabinet members and he never did find those few reliable friends in government whom Presidents before and after him have found so helpful. His term was short and is forever linked to the Compromise of 1850, which the

President opposed consistently until the day he died.

Back in 1820 during the administration of James Monroe, the Missouri Compromise had kept the scales even between free and slave states. It had not, of course, solved the issue of slavery. That would take a civil war. But now the slavery issue was very much alive again in Congress with the prospect of California and New Mexico entering the Union. Above all, Taylor did not want a national debate over slavery. So, he wanted California admitted without first becoming a territory. That would mean that Congress would not be involved in deciding whether it should be slave or free. The new state itself would decide. The same for New Mexico.

The South was horrified by Taylor's attitude. Surely California would become a free state, thereby upsetting the slave-free balance. It looked like Congress and Taylor were about to lock horns.

Onto the battlefield stepped the Great Compromiser, Senator Henry Clay of Kentucky. He suggested the following plan: Texas

In this contemporary color engraving, Senator Henry Clay (Kentucky) is shown offering the Compromise of 1850 to the Senate on February 5. The California Compromise gave the nation 11 years of peace prior to the Civil War.

would get $10 million to give up claims to New Mexican territory; California would enter as a free state; the question of slavery in both the New Mexico and Utah territories would be left to each of them to settle; the western boundary for Texas would be set a little farther east than Texas had wanted; there would be no slave trade in Washington, D.C.; and a stronger law would be passed concerning the return of runaway slaves. The last point was intended to appease the Southerners, who had long claimed that the government gave them no help in returning what they believed to be their rightful property.

Clay won support from many in Congress for his plan, but the President proved surprisingly stubborn. He was having none of the Compromise of 1850, and if the South didn't like it and tried to pull out of the Union, he would personally lead the U.S. Army against them!

The Senate debate over the Compromise of 1850 lasted seven months! Almost everyone had something to say, including one of the great patriots, the ailing, elderly Daniel Webster. In his last impressive speech, he implored the Senate to hear his cause for "I speak today for the preservation of the Union." This great Yankee statesman was eloquent in his defense of Clay's proposals. Although his speech won him no friends with antislavery people, it did edge the two sides toward compromise. As the months followed and the deadlock continued, both North and South began to feel that the only way out of this dilemma was, indeed, a coming together.

The President, however, stayed firm. If passed, he would veto the bill. That Congress could override his veto by the required two-thirds majority was doubtful.

Sometimes fate has a way of stepping in against all odds. The Fourth of July 1850 dawned hot and sunny in the nation's capital. Very hot and sunny. Ceremonies were to be held around the still unfinished tribute to the first President, the Washington Monument. President Taylor, of course, attended, sitting for hours in the blazing sun. By the time he returned to the White House, he was unbearably hot and thirsty. According to the tale, he immediately consumed great amounts of raw cherries and iced milk. Within two days he was ill with an extreme gastric upset. He died unexpectedly on July 9, 1850. Thousands of mourners lined the route to his grave in Jefferson County, Kentucky, and the procession of 100 carriages stretched for two miles.

Less than three months after Taylor's death, the Compromise of 1850 was passed and became law. There was much relief that the "Union had been saved." Of course, it had not. The clash between slave and free factions had only been put off once again. But the wounds were still there, compromises were harder to reach, and the time of the inevitable clash was growing closer.

Was Zachary Taylor a good President? He was tough to be sure and far more strong-willed than might have been thought. People's biggest criticism of him was his lack of political and administrative experience. He was a national hero and very popular. He is generally regarded as naive in government but a well-intentioned person. Historians do not place Old Rough and Ready high on the list in presidential influence and ability. But perhaps, far more than anyone realized, Taylor was able to stand on his own two feet, even in the White House.

Names in the News in Taylor's Time

Lewis Cass (1782–1866):

New Hampshire-born lawyer, governor of Michigan Territory, secretary of war under Jackson. Democratic presidential candidate (1848), but for Van Buren and slavery issue may have become the twelfth President instead of Taylor.

Winfield Scott (1786–1866):

Virginia-born, physically impressive (6'6"), pompous brigadier general, rival to Taylor; brilliant strategist in Mexican campaign. Whig presidential candidate, defeated by Franklin Pierce (1852); retired 1861.

Chapter Seven

Millard Fillmore Who?

Millard Fillmore (1850-1853)

Surely no chief executive has had more jokes made about his name than the thirteenth President of the United States—Millard Fillmore of Cayuga County, New York. But at least his name is remembered longer than his two years and 236 days in office. Actually, Fillmore was an effective administrator and a good public servant. But fate had made him President in 1850. Perhaps no one who took the presidential oath of office, of whatever name, could have stemmed the tide of events. Certainly Fillmore could not. Like Pierce and Buchanan who followed him, Fillmore did not see that strong leadership was needed. It was useless to apply a small bandage to the gaping wounds that now divided North and South.

Fillmore's actions, strong and weak, good and bad, were lost in the bitterness and anger of coming war, in the bloodshed and pain of the war itself, and in the chaos and scars that followed it. In all that, it was easy to forget the time between 1850 and 1853 and, later, to ask: Millard Fillmore who?

On July 9, 1850, for the second time in the nation's young history, a President died in office. This time, however, Vice President Fillmore was not as shocked as Vice President Tyler had been upon hearing the news of Harrison's death. Fillmore had been told a few hours earlier that President Zachary Taylor was gravely ill. But if not shocked, Fillmore was certainly overwhelmed. It is said he locked his door and spent a long and sleepless night. The next morning he took the oath as the thirteenth President of the United States. He was 50 years old.

Fillmore was born in a log cabin to poor, hardworking parents, Nathaniel and Phoebe Fillmore, of Locke Township, Cayuga County, New York. They gave their second child and first son his mother's maiden name. He was born on January 7, 1800. In all, Millard's parents raised a family of six boys and three girls.

Education was as scarce as money on the Fillmore farm. Young Millard had very little formal schooling and did not even see a dictionary until he was 17 years old. Shortly thereafter, he managed to attend school for six months. Even when he became President, Fillmore never tried to hide his lack of formal schooling.

Formal schooling or not, Millard was a bright lad, and at age 18, he was hired by a local lawyer. In 1823, he opened his own law office near Buffalo, New York. By age 30, he had grown tall and husky, a witty, deep-voiced, dignified man whom most regarded as quite handsome. In 1826, he married Abigail Powers, a minister's daughter. They would have two children.

Fillmore got his political feet wet by joining the Antimasonic party in the late 1820s. It was organized against the Masons, or Freemasons. Not a religious organization, the secret society of Freemasons adopted many of the ceremonies of ancient religious orders. This male-only group had through the years been charged with prejudice against Catholics, nonwhites, and Jews, as well as with economic and social conspiracies. Today's Masons strongly deny any prejudices or conspiracies. In 1834 the Antimasons joined the Whig party and Fillmore became a Whig.

When Harrison was elected as the first Whig President in 1841, Fillmore held a powerful post in the U.S. House of Representatives. He was chairman of the Ways and Means Committee, which is concerned with raising revenues. The Whigs began to eye him more closely. He was popular, handsome, squeaky clean, hardworking, and from a state with a large population. But he shocked his colleagues by refusing to run for reelection in 1842. Fillmore had his eye on the Senate. However, by 1844, friends had persuaded him to run for governor of New York. It was a bad time to be a Whig, and Fillmore lost his first election.

Politics is nothing, however, if not ups and downs, and by 1848, things were looking up for the Whigs. Popular Old Rough and Ready Taylor was their choice for President. Henry Clay of Kentucky supported Millard Fillmore for the second spot.

Once in the White House, Taylor became embroiled in the difficult issue of the Compromise of 1850. Clay had proposed it as a way to settle the deadlock between slave and free states over the admission of California and New Mexico and the dispute over Texas. The President was against the Compromise. As the debate in Congress headed for its seventh month, Vice President Fillmore was worried. What if Congress deadlocked on a vote? That was certainly possible. It would mean that the vice president—Fillmore—would cast the deciding vote. Secession was always a threat. The very Union was at stake. What to do?

Before the Fourth of July, Fillmore called on the President. Said the vice president: "If I should feel it my duty to vote for it [meaning the Compromise, which the President opposed], as I might, I wish you to understand that it is not out of any hostility to you or your administration, but the vote will be given, because I deem it for the interests of the country."

His conscience clear, Fillmore went home for the holiday. But, of course, he never had to cast that deciding vote. On July 9, Taylor suddenly died and Millard Fillmore was now President. The Compromise of 1850 was passed, and the crisis was past— for the moment.

The Fillmores moved into the White House, probably with some misgivings on the part of the First Lady. Already frail and sickly, she soon realized that living in the President's mansion could be hazardous to one's health. In fact, just living in Washington, D.C., could be dangerous to one's health. The nearby Potomac River was a hotbed of mosquitoes, and the threat of malaria was very real. The White House itself was big, drafty, and damp. Meals were cooked on a primitive open fireplace. One of the changes Fillmore made was to install a small closed-in cooking stove.

The credit for an even more lasting change in White House living, however, must go to the President's wife. A former schoolteacher, Abigail Fillmore was horrified when she walked into her new home. There was not one single book in the entire mansion! Taking matters into her own hands, she pressured Congress for some money, with which she established the first White House Library. Her initial purchases were sets of Charles Dickens and William Thackeray, some history books, and a dictionary.

Abigail Powers Fillmore

Meanwhile, the President was busy with the Compromise of 1850. It contained these important items: California was admitted as a free state. New Mexico and Utah were organized as territories with no federal ban on slavery, understanding being that the popular vote of the people in those areas would eventually determine the slavery status. The slave trade was forbidden in the District of Columbia, but slavery itself was permitted!

Fillmore was worried about the Fugitive Slave Act, which was part of the Compromise of 1850. It had been included to appease the South. Ever since the first such law, in 1793, northern states increasingly had refused to assist in the return of runaway slaves. This allowed a small abolitionist force to hide slaves rather easily and help them escape from the South to the North or even into Canada before the Civil War. This secret and informal network was known as the "Underground Railroad."

Although Fillmore was antislavery, once convinced that the Fugitive Slave Act was constitutional, he had no choice but to sign it. And sign it he did, thereby making both North and South unhappy. Northerners were already in a stir over Harriet

This escape from the tyrannies of slavery, entitled "A Ride for Liberty,"
was painted by American artist Eastman Johnson in 1893.

Beecher Stowe's novel, a harsh indictment of slavery entitled
Uncle Tom's Cabin. They became even more angry over the Slave
Act's harshness and vowed further defiance. Even though the
South wanted some help in this matter, it was convinced that the
1850 act only meant more federal interference.

Like the quiet before a storm, things calmed down for a bit.
The President turned to other matters. He took steps to improve
trade with Japan. Fillmore also approved federal grants for railroad construction to open the West. He began the delicate task of
restoring friendly relations with Mexico as well as other lands
south of the border.

By election time, 1852, the Whig party was badly split.
Although Fillmore's name was placed in nomination, the party
turned to General Winfield Scott, on the fifty-third ballot! Scott
and the Whigs were doomed, losing to Democrat Franklin
Pierce. The Whigs disappeared from the political scene.

But Fillmore did not—quite. His beloved Abigail died in early
1853 and he plunged himself totally into politics. By 1856, the
former President was nominated as the candidate of the Know-
Nothings. Officially called the American party, this was one of the
more bizarre groups in U.S. politics. A strong anti-immigrant,
anti-Catholic feeling had sprung up by the mid-1800s, primarily

against Irish and German immigrants. U.S. Protestants claimed their economic security and moral order were threatened. In 1850, they formed the secret Order of the Star-Spangled Banner in New York City. When asked about their group, members were supposed to answer that they knew nothing—hence the name.

In a Know-Nothing cartoon, Irish and German immigrants, portrayed by Irish whisky and German beer, were charged with stealing American elections and running big city political machines.

The Know-Nothings candidate won only the state of Maryland as Democrat James Buchanan beat out Republican John C. Fremont in the election of 1856. Politics was finally over for Millard Fillmore. He married wealthy widow Caroline McIntosh in 1858 and they retired to Buffalo, New York, where they once had the honor of entertaining Abraham Lincoln.

The thirteenth President of the United States died of a stroke on March 8, 1874. He is buried in Buffalo, where his gravestone marks a competent leader who is still known or unknown by many as Millard Fillmore who?

Names in the News in Fillmore's Time

Horace Greeley (1811–1872):

New Hampshire-born journalist. Founded *New Yorker* magazine with Jonas Winchester (1834) and *New York Tribune* newspaper (1841). Lost to U.S. Grant in presidential election of 1872. The advice to seek fame and fortune in the phrase "Go west, young man" is generally attributed to Greeley, who published it in the *Tribune*. However, it was first said by John Babson Lane Soule in the *Terre Haute* (Indiana) *Express*, which Greeley himself later acknowledged.

Jenny (Johanna Maria) Lind (1820–1887):

Known as the Swedish nightingale for her unmatched soprano voice. Toast of the opera world. Brought to America by P.T. Barnum to tour with the circus (1850–1852).

Herman Melville (1819–1891):

American novelist, born New York City; ran away to sea and wrote several novels of his experiences. Most famous for the classic *Moby Dick* (1851).

Harriet Ross Tubman (c.1820–1913):

Fugitive slave, nicknamed Moses for helping more than 300 slaves to freedom on Underground Railroad after 1850. Union spy and scout during Civil War.

This caricature of Horace Greeley was made by Thomas Nast in 1872.

Chapter Eight

Pierce: In the Hurricane's Eye

Franklin Pierce (1853-1857)

*W*as the fourteenth President of the United States the wrong man at the wrong time? He began his term with a tragedy that doomed his personal life and ended it with a tragedy that doomed his administration. Imagine the whole fight over slavery as a brewing storm. It had been gathering energy for years before Pierce entered the White House. But he became President believing in the fragile calm that gripped the nation after the Compromise of 1850. Franklin Pierce now stood in the eye of a hurricane, not seeing or feeling what would soon sweep him away.

At age 48, he was the youngest man to sit in the White House until John F. Kennedy. But Franklin Pierce was a throwback to earlier, calmer times. His heroes were Madison and Monroe and other Founding Fathers. His total commitment was to preserve the Union. He believed in the Compromise of 1850. Even though he was a Northerner himself, he never understood the passionate feelings of those who believed slavery to be an evil institution. Consequently, he never understood why antislavery advocates were stirring up so much trouble. Handsome and charming, he was, even in the mid-1800s, old-fashioned. Always eager to please others, he was more a follower than a leader. He died in 1869, not quite 65 years old, broken by the tragedy of his life and depressed by its failures.

Pierce is the only President to come from the small state of New Hampshire. He was born in Hillsboro on November 23, 1804, the sixth of seven children. His father, Benjamin, was a general in the Revolution and became New Hampshire's governor, giving young Franklin an introduction to politics.

By 1824, Pierce had graduated from Bowdoin College in Maine, becoming a lawyer at age 22 and a state legislator at age 24. His upward climb took him to the U.S. Senate in 1837. But five years later, it looked like his promising career was over. Pierce had married Jane Means Appleton in 1834. She was the daughter of the Bowdoin College president and almost fanatically religious. Perhaps that's why she hated both politics and Washington, D.C. In an effort to please his bride, Pierce gave up his Senate seat and they returned to New Hampshire where he went into private law practice. He did take time out for the Mexican War in 1847. Commissioned a brigadier general, he fought under Winfield Scott in the battle at Mexico City.

By election time 1852, Franklin Pierce must have seemed the darkest of dark horses. He certainly did not appear to be a front-runner. Although he had kept his hand in local politics, who knew much about this small-time lawyer from a small-size state? Almost no one. In view of his wife's feelings, Pierce certainly couldn't behave as though he truly *wanted* the nomination.

But politics is a strange game. This time Pierce was in the right place with the right attitude. Even though neither North nor South was totally happy with the Compromise of 1850, each side *wanted* to believe that it would work and solve everyone's problems. Pierce was enthusiastically for the Compromise. Add to that the fact that the Democrats could not seem to get their act together and agree on a candidate. After 49 ballots, a weary convention, wanting to go home, settled on handsome, unknown, obscure Franklin Pierce of New Hampshire.

Pierce received the news of his unexpected nomination quietly—probably because his wife fainted. Their adored

11-year-old son Bennie later wrote to his mother: "I hope he won't be elected for I should not like to be at Washington and I know you would not either." Alas for Bennie, he never did make it to Washington, although his parents did.

The Whigs put up General Winfield Scott. With Scott's defeat, the party itself would soon disappear. Pierce took 27 states to Scott's four, with 254 electoral votes against 42. It was a landslide for the dark horse.

Pierce's running mate was Southerner William R. King, who died a month after Inauguration Day. The office of vice president remained vacant throughout Pierce's term. With the prevailing attitude of the country toward that position, it is possible that no one noticed. Franklin Pierce, quietly elated, and Jane Pierce, clearly reluctant, began to make plans for his inauguration in Washington on March 4, 1853. Then,

tragedy struck. That January they traveled by train from Boston to Concord, New Hampshire. Their son Bennie was with them. The railroad car in which they were riding jumped the track, leaving the parents unhurt but killing Bennie.

It was a tragedy from which neither Franklin nor his wife would ever recover. Having lost one baby at birth and another at a very young age, they regarded their only surviving child as the light of their lives. Jane Pierce took Bennie's death as a religious sign. Always melancholy and withdrawn, she was now totally grief stricken and rarely

Jane Means Appleton Pierce is shown in this circa 1850 photo with her son Benjamin.

made public appearances. In fact, she was not well enough to witness her husband's inauguration as the fourteenth President of the United States.

As for the new President, he never seemed able to throw off the guilt he felt because of Bennie's death. His inauguration was quiet and restrained, without an inaugural ball in deference to his loss. His speech, however, was positive and spirited, for Pierce was a fluent orator. He was also the first President to memorize his inaugural speech. In the afternoon, well-wishers dropped by the White House to congratulate the new President. A few hours later, the place was full of unwashed dishes and disarranged furniture. The servants had gone home before the guests. That night, Pierce and his private secretary, Sidney Webster, carried a candle around the darkened and deserted White House looking for a place to sleep. Is this any way to treat a President?

Actually, in 1853, it was. Incredible as it may seem by modern standards, becoming President of the United States didn't always bring the personal attention the public is used to today. It also generally did not bring personal wealth. Depending on its mood, Congress appropriated money for furnishings and upkeep on the mansion. It paid the President $25,000, which most of the country regarded as more than adequate. And perhaps it was. However, out of that the President had to hire and pay for his own household help and supplies, plus all family daily needs, even official duty expenses. In other words, if President Pierce invited a foreign head of state to dinner, which would have been a rare event at the time, Pierce—not the United States—paid for it!

It was not until Ulysses Grant's second term that the President earned $50,000. Of course, in 1873, that was quite a huge amount. It went up to $75,000 for William H. Taft in 1909 and $100,000 for Harry S Truman in 1949. Since 1969, the President's salary has been a taxable $200,000, plus a $50,000 expense account. There are, of course, other benefits.

There were some changes in the White House during Pierce's time. The first central furnace was installed in 1853, presumably clearing up complaints of perpetual dampness. And as a sure sign that life in the United States was becoming more complicated, President Pierce was the first to hire a full-time bodyguard.

Pierce settled in to govern and was soon involved in what has been called the great tragedy of his administration—the Kansas-Nebraska Act.

In January 1854, Democratic Senator Stephen A. Douglas of Illinois submitted a bill to organize land west of Missouri and Iowa into territories and eventually states. The land in question, called the Nebraska country, had been set aside for Native Americans in 1830, but few in Congress objected to the bill on that ground. Instead, the old question of slavery cropped up. The Missouri Compromise had closed this land to slavery. If Douglas's bill passed, wouldn't that compromise in effect be repealed?

The South indeed called for outright repeal. Douglas made two changes in the Kansas-Nebraska bill to appease the South. Although not repealing the Missouri Compromise outright, the new bill declared

Senator Stephen Arnold Douglas (Democrat, Illinois) in a photograph circa 1852.

it "void and inoperative." The Kansas-Nebraska Act would let the people in the new territory decide on slavery for themselves. This policy was known as "popular sovereignty." The revised bill also divided the Nebraska country into two parts. The northern part would be called Nebraska and the southern would be called Kansas. This division made it likely that Kansas would be a slave state, since it was immediately to the west of the slave state of Missouri.

Pierce was not happy about the revised bill. He wanted the Supreme Court to decide outright on the Missouri Compromise. He believed the Court would declare it unconstitutional. But Douglas's concessions won the support of most Southerners. So Pierce gave in and supported the revised bill. The Kansas-Nebraska bill became law on May 30, 1854, and Pierce thought he had a victory.

He may have, but it caused a tremendous rift in the Democratic party. All the old bitterness over slavery resurfaced. Most surprised was Senator Douglas. He personally did not care one way or the other about slavery and thought he had saved the Union. Instead, he was mobbed by abolitionists in his own state. More importantly, the Kansas-Nebraska Act strengthened a brand new political party—the Republicans.

What the Kansas-Nebraska Act also did was to produce "Bleeding Kansas." The new territory immediately became the focus of a kind of civil war. Proslavery factions flocked in from the South. After organizing a convention and forging a constitution, they set up a government capital at Lecompton, Kansas. The territorial governor, fearing for his life, recognized this new capital. Therefore, Pierce did, too. Antislavery settlers flocked in from the North and set up a government at Topeka. Now, Kansas had just what it didn't need—two capitals and two governments.

Uncertain of what to do with this mess, Pierce hesitated. In 1856, a small war broke out and 200 men died. The President then

Free state forces in Kansas Territory received weapons such as this cannon from abolitionists determined not to let the region be controlled by proponents of slavery.

sent in John W. Geary as governor, who called in federal troops. Bleeding Kansas bled no more, but tempers were high and would remain so. When Kansas became a state in 1861, it outlawed slavery but excluded free blacks.

His party split, tempers raging, Pierce turned to other matters. He was successful in that Commodore Matthew Perry, already sent to Japan by Fillmore, arranged a treaty to open up trade with the United States. A dispute over North American fishing rights between Great Britain and the United States was settled. Pierce was also very much interested in adding territory to the country. However, he failed in the passage of a treaty to annex Hawaii. He also failed to acquire the island of Cuba, one of his prime objectives, which he saw as becoming part of the southern slave system. For this task, he sent a bungling minister, Pierre Soulé, to Spain. Soulé was expected to get Cuba by fair means or foul, including threat of war. But he made so many mistakes, including challenging the Spanish ambassador to a duel, that the New York *Herald* wrote: "We wanted an Ambassador there, we have sent a matador."

Still, Pierce persisted. What would happen if the United States invaded the island? The bumbling Soulé was instructed by Secretary of State William L. Marcy to find out, through the U.S. ministers in London and Paris, how those countries would respond to an American invasion. Apparently, the ministers did not understand Soulé's message. Instead of replying to the question, the ministers sent a message to Marcy from Ostend, Belgium. It said, in effect, that the United States should offer $120 million for Cuba, and take the island by force if refused.

When word of the so-called Ostend Manifesto reached the public, there was a huge uproar. Northerners called it a plot to add another slave state to the Union. The North got so angry that Pierce had to call off the plan—for the time being.

For all his expansionist dreams, Pierce was able to add only about 40,000 square miles of desert to the United States.

Diplomat and railroad promoter James Gadsden negotiated the Gadsden Purchase in 1853. For $10 million, Mexico gave up land in what are now New Mexico and Arizona. This cleared the way for a transcontinental railroad through the South.

Franklin Pierce would have liked another term, but Bleeding Kansas and his turmoil-ridden party did him in. He continued to uphold the rights of slave states as constitutional and he continued to regard the abolitionists as fanatics. Not surprisingly, northern Democrats had no use for him, and the South knew he couldn't win without the North. So, the party nominated James Buchanan instead.

After spending two years with his wife in Europe, Pierce returned to find himself back in favor with the Democrats. It is said that absence makes the heart grow fonder. This time around, however, he said no to another try at the presidency. He turned bitter when the new Republican party put Abraham Lincoln in the White House in 1861. He turned increasingly bitter through the war that followed. On July 4, 1863, he spoke to Democrats in Concord, New Hampshire, condemning this "fearful, fruitless, fatal Civil War." While the crowd still gathered, word came of the tremendous victory for the North at Gettysburg.

Jane Pierce died in 1864. Franklin's death came five years later, on October 8, at his home in Concord, New Hampshire, where he is buried.

With Franklin Pierce ended the formative years of the United States. What would follow would be growth and expansion, from midcentury to end. But first would come what had been avoided for so long, the American Civil War. So devastating was this conflict that it tore brother from brother, family from family, and nearly destroyed the marvelous experiment in democracy begun nearly three-quarters of a century before. Pierce was powerless to stop the tide of onrushing war. He was a man broken not by the terrible strength of a hurricane, but by standing, unbent, in its eye.

Names in the News in Pierce's Time

Ralph Waldo Emerson (1803–1882):

Boston-born poet and essayist, Harvard graduate. Gained international reputation with publication of *Essays* (1841, 1844). Delivered antislavery speeches.

Nathaniel Hawthorne (1804–1864):

American novelist, born Salem, Massachusetts. Fellow student with Pierce at Bowdoin College. Most famous for *The Scarlet Letter* (1850) and *The House of the Seven Gables* (1851).

William L. Marcy (1786–1857):

Born Sturbridge, Massachusetts. U.S. senator; secretary of war under Pierce. Coined the phrase "spoils system" (1832), saying there was "nothing wrong in the rule that to the victor belong the spoils."

Matthew C. Perry (1794–1858):

American naval officer, born Newport, Rhode Island. Sent by Fillmore to open trade with Japan; negotiated treaty during Pierce's administration.

Commodore Matthew C. Perry is caricatured unflatteringly by a Japanese artist around 1853.

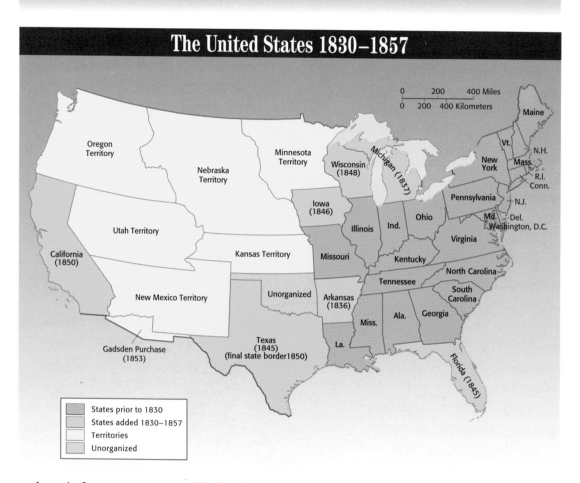

The United States 1830–1857

0   200   400 Miles

0   200   400 Kilometers

Oregon Territory

Minnesota Territory

Wisconsin (1848)

Michigan (1837)

Maine

Vt.

N.H.

New York

Mass.

R.I.

Conn.

Nebraska Territory

Iowa (1846)

Ohio

Pennsylvania

N.J.

Md.

Del.

Washington, D.C.

Utah Territory

Illinois

Ind.

Virginia

California (1850)

Kansas Territory

Missouri

Kentucky

North Carolina

New Mexico Territory

Unorganized

Arkansas (1836)

Tennessee

South Carolina

Miss.

Ala.

Georgia

Gadsden Purchase (1853)

Texas (1845) (final state border 1850)

La.

Florida (1845)

States prior to 1830
States added 1830–1857
Territories
Unorganized

A total of seven states were added to the United States in this twenty-eight-year period, and the country spread from coast to coast.

Important Facts and Events in the Terms
of Presidents Seven Through Fourteen

7. Andrew Jackson (1829–1837)

Democratic party; age at inauguration, 61
Born: Waxhaw, South Carolina, March 15, 1767
Died: Nashville,Tennessee, June 8, 1845
Education; occupation: Self-educated; lawyer, soldier
Military service: Major general Tennessee militia, 1802–1812;
    major general U.S. Army, 1814–1821
Family: Rachel Donelson Robards (married 1791)
Important events during Jackson's terms:

    1831: Nat Turner's Rebellion, slave uprising in Virginia

    1832: Federal tax "nullified" in South Carolina.

    1835: War with the Seminoles

    1836: Texas declares independence; Battle of the Alamo;
            Arkansas becomes 25th state.

    1837: Michigan becomes 26th state.

8. Martin Van Buren (1837–1841)

Democratic party; age at inauguration, 54
Born: Kinderhook, New York, December 5, 1782
Died: Kinderhook, New York, July 24, 1862
Education; occupation: Common (public) schools; lawyer
Family: Hannah Hoes (married 1807);
    children: Abraham, John, Martin, Smith Thompson
Important events during Van Buren's term:

    1837: Economic "Panic of 1837";
            Seminoles lose battle at Okeechobee, Florida;
            Canadian Rebellion

    1840: "Independent Treasury" established.

9. William Henry Harrison (1841)

Whig party; age at inauguration, 68
Born: Berkeley, Virginia, February 9, 1773
Died: Washington, D.C., April 4, 1841
Education; occupation: Hampden-Sydney College ; soldier
Military service: Major general U.S. Army
Family: Anna Symmes (married 1795); children: Elizabeth, John, Cleves,
   Lucy, William, John Scott, Benjamin, Mary, Carter, Anna, James
Important event during Harrison's term:
   1841: Died in office.

10. John Tyler (1841–1845)

Whig party; age at inauguration, 51
Born: Greenway, Virginia, March 19, 1790
Died: Richmond, Virginia, January 18, 1862
Education; occupation: College of William and Mary; lawyer
Family: Letitia Christian (married 1813); Julia Gardiner (married 1844);
   children: Mary, Robert, John, Letitia, Elizabeth, Alice, Tazewell, David,
   John Alexander, Julia, Lachlan, Lyon, Robert, Pearl
Important events during Tyler's term:
   1842: Maine boundary settled; Seminole War ended.
   1844: Treaty of Wanghia signed with China.
   1845: Florida becomes 27th state.

11. James Knox Polk (1845–1849)

Democratic party; age at inauguration, 49
Born: Mecklenburg County, North Carolina, November 2, 1795
Died: Nashville, Tennessee, June 15, 1849
Education; occupation: University of North Carolina; lawyer
Family: Sarah Childress (married 1824)
Important events during Polk's term:
   1845: Texas becomes 28th state.
   1846: War with Mexico; Oregon Treaty signed with Great Britain;
          Wilmot Proviso; Iowa becomes 29th state.
   1848: California Gold Rush; peace treaty signed with Mexico;
          Wisconsin becomes 30th state.
   1849: Department of the Interior created.

12. Zachary Taylor (1849–1850)

Whig party, age at inauguration, 64

Born: Orange County, Virginia, November 24, 1784

Died: Washington, D.C., July 9, 1850

Education; occupation: Common (public) schools; soldier

Military service: Major general U.S. Army

Family: Margaret Smith (married 1810)

Important events during Taylor's term:

    1849: California Gold Rush

    1850: Died in office.

13. Millard Fillmore (1850–1853)

Whig party; age at inauguration, 50

Born: Cayuga County, New York, January 7, 1800

Died: Buffalo, New York, March 8, 1874

Education; occupation: Common (public) schools; lawyer

Family: Abigail Powers (married 1826), Caroline McIntosh (married 1858);
    children: Millard, Mary

Important events during Fillmore's term:

    1850: Compromise of 1850; California becomes 31st state.

    1852: Commodore Perry sails for Japan; *Uncle Tom's Cabin* published.

14. Franklin Pierce (1853–1857)

Democratic party; age at inauguration, 48

Born: Hillsboro, New Hampshire, November 13, 1804

Died: Concord, New Hampshire, October 8, 1869

Education; occupation: Bowdoin College; lawyer

Military service: Brigadier general U.S. Army

Family: Jane Appleton (married 1834); children: Frank, Benjamin

Important events during Pierce's term:

    1854: Treaty with Japan; Kansas-Nebraska Act; Gadsden Purchase

    1856: Kansas "bleeds."

Glossary

annexation The act of adding or uniting, often used when referring to territory that is added to a country.

compromise A settlement of differences, usually brought about by two sides giving in a little to reach agreement.

depression In economics, a period of low activity marked by rising levels of unemployment.

frontiersman One who lives or works in a region of generally undeveloped territory; in early U.S. history, generally referred to someone who helped settle the West.

impeachment The act of charging a public official with a crime.

landmark In the historic sense, a structure or building preserved because of historic significance, as Jackson's Tennessee home, The Hermitage, is now a landmark.

monopoly Exclusive possession, as, for instance, the manufacturing and or selling of a product by only one party.

mudslinging Using vicious or nasty words or phrases against a political opponent in a campaign.

nullification When a state tries to prevent the operation of a federal law within its own territory.

platform Statement of principles, beliefs, or plans adopted by a political party or candidate.

pocket veto When a President neither signs nor vetoes a bill, after a specified time it does not become law; the President is said to have used a pocket veto.

spoils system Practice of giving public offices to members of the victorious political party regardless of merit.

Further Reading

Blumberg, Rhoda. *Commodore Perry in the Land of the Shogun.* Lothrop, Lee & Shepard, 1985

Brown, Fern G. *Franklin Pierce: Fourteenth President of the United States.* Garrett, 1989

Civiklik, Robert. *Tecumseh: Shawnee Rebel.* Chelsea House, 1994

Coil, Suzanne M. *Harriet Beecher Stowe.* Franklin Watts, 1993.

Collins, David R. *Zachary Taylor: Twelfth President of the United States.* Garrett, 1989

Falk, Lucille. *John Tyler: Tenth President of the United States.* Garrett, 1990

Feinberg, Barbara S. *American Political Scandals Past and Present.* Franklin Watts, 1992

Fremon, David. *Trail of Tears.* Silver Burdett, 1994

Greenblatt, Miriam. *James K. Polk: Eleventh President of the United States.* Garrett, 1988

Harness, Cheryl. *The Amazing Impossible Erie Canal.* Simon & Schuster, 1995

James, Marquis. *The Raven: A Biography of Sam Houston.* University of Texas Press, 1988

Law, Kevin J. *Millard Fillmore: Thirteenth President of the United States.* Garrett, 1990

Lindop, Edmund. *Presidents by Accident.* Franklin Watts, 1991

Mayo, Edith, ed. *The Smithsonian Book of the First Ladies: Their Lives, Times, and Issues.* Holt, 1996

Meltzer, Milton. *Andrew Jackson: And His America.* Franklin Watts, 1993

Mills, Bronwyn. *The Mexican War.* Facts on File, 1992

Ragsdale, Crystal. *The Women and Children of the Alamo.* State House Press, 1994

Steffoff, Rebecca. *William Henry Harrison: Ninth President of the United States.* Garrett, 1990

Van Leeuwen, Jean. *Bound for Oregon.* Dial/Penguin, 1994

Welles, Ted. *Van Buren, Wizard of O.K. and 8th U.S.A. President.* Oceanus Institute, 1987

Index